Jan, 2000
Dear Curtis,
Sorry I couldn't get it
autographed for you
will autograph it myse o

Enjoy Reading
Love Always
Cheryl

(How's that? 😊)
(see next page)

Sixty Years
on the Back Foot

Sixty Years on the Back Foot

The Cricketing Life of
Sir Clyde Walcott

CLYDE WALCOTT

WITH BRIAN SCOVELL

VICTOR GOLLANCZ
LONDON

First published in Great Britain in 1999 by Victor Gollancz
An imprint of Orion Books Ltd
Wellington House, 125 Strand, London WC2R 0BB

A CIP catlogue record for this book
is available from the British Library

ISBN 0 575 06755 1

Typeset by Selwood Systems, Midsomer Norton
Printed and bound by Butler & Tanner Ltd, Frome and London

Contents

Foreword

EVERTON DECOURCEY WEEKES

Clyde Walcott would have been a great cricketer in any era. I am
sure of that. Just as Joe Louis or Muhammad Ali would have been
great boxers at any time in the history of that sport.

The boxing analogy is apt because Clyde had a powerful phys-
ique and his batting was based on power and strength. He hit the
ball harder than any of us. He had a unique style, a double backlift
that encouraged some bowlers early in his career to believe that
they had a chance of bowling him before his bat came down.
They were to be disappointed.

It was amazing that Clyde, Frank Worrell and myself were all
born within a mile of the Kensington Oval cricket ground in
Barbados. I first met him at the age of sixteen when we played
together in a trial game. He was a huge man, towering over me,
and was renowned as an outstanding all-round sportsman. He
played football, tennis, table tennis and was a long jumper, high
jumper and hurdler. He was so good on the sports field that he
had no time for passing examinations. We had that in common.
Frank was the cleverest of the Three Ws and I believe that, had
he not died of leukaemia at the tragically early age of forty-two,
he would have become a governor-general somewhere.

Although we achieved so many feats together, we were never
rivals. We were close friends, sharing a room whenever it was
possible because we liked each other's company.

Clyde became an administrator, serving on a number of boards and committees, eventually becoming chairman of the International Cricket Council. He has probably put more back into the game than any cricketer of similar stature.

I suspect the achievement that has given him greatest satisfaction was the way he revitalized cricket in British Guiana as it was then and helped in the development of such brilliant players as Rohan Kanhai, Basil Butcher, Joe Solomon, Alvin Kallicharran, Roy Fredericks and Lance Gibbs.

Few cricketers have maintained such a prominent and successful role in world cricket as Clyde Walcott, my great friend.

Barbados 1998

1 'You Will Never Make a Living from Cricket!'

The world is full of schoolteachers who have issued dire warnings to their pupils about failure to pass their exams. When I was fourteen a teacher named Querée at Harrison College in Barbados said to me, 'You will have to do better at your schoolwork because you can't make a living out of cricket.'

I did not pass a single examination but I became a useful cricketer. Some years later, after my highest score of 314 not out, I met Mr Querée, who was an Englishman, and he greeted me with a broad smile. 'You made me eat my hat,' he said.

My first memory of playing cricket was when I was aged three. I was given a small, cut-down bat and used to take part in the cricket games in the backyard of our house, a fairly large property which had been a plantation manager's house. My father Frank was employed as an engineer at the *Barbados Advocate*, the local daily newspaper. He loved cricket, as do nearly all Bajans, but he was a better tennis player. The backyard, some forty yards by twenty-five, was our Kensington Oval (the real one was a few hundred yards down the road). Our Oval had a dirt surface and we played with a piece of rounded stone wrapped in cloth and bound with twine, or a breadfruit from one of the trees. At Christmas my father would buy us a composition ball.

My brother Keith, who is two years older than me, never wanted anything for Christmas other than a bat or a ball. And I was the same. When I was older my father brought a bat back from his trip to England for Keith and a violin for me. He thought I was more interested in music. Like every West Indian, I liked music ... but not as much as cricket. I envied Keith's bat.

There were as many as eight people living in our house: my father, my mother Ruth, Keith and myself and various uncles and an aunt. My Uncle Ernest was one of the founders of the Empire Cricket Club, one of the top clubs in Barbados. Another uncle was Harold Walcott, the Test umpire, but he did not live with us.

No one coached us, although we obviously had a lot of advice. We learned from watching others, players like Derek Sealy, one of our teachers who represented the West Indies. There were not just boys playing in our backyard, but men, some of them leading cricketers from the club sides. The standard was high. There was a galvanized fence around the yard and we also used a piece of galvanized steel as the stumps. You knew if you were out because the ball would hit the metal with a loud twang. For most of my childhood years we played for five or six hours a day until it became dark. There was a short break of a few weeks when we played more football, but cricket was the main sport.

My mother was a Methodist and every Sunday Keith and I had to attend Sunday school. We had to behave, otherwise we would be denied our weekend treat, which was our regular bike ride.

Although we were only a quarter of a mile from Kensington Oval, I was almost nine before I was taken to see my first Test match. George Headley, the batsman from Jamaica who was rated the best in the West Indies, scored 44 out of 102. In a low-scoring match, the West Indies declaring at 51 for six in their second innings, England won by four wickets. Walter Hammond was England's leading scorer with 43 and 29 not out. I didn't have a hero in those days. We preferred playing to watching heroes.

I was born on 17 January 1926 at the family house, and I believe I was delivered by the same midwife who delivered Everton

Weekes and Frank Worrell. She was a small lady who delivered all the babies in the area. Barbados has a strong Scottish influence and my mother had Scottish blood, which is probably why I was named Clyde. I have not been able to find out why I was also given the name Leopold.

Walcott is a common name in Barbados and in the latest telephone directory there are 293 listed, compared to 239 Weekeses and 245 Worrells. We were all born within a square mile of the Kensington Oval and I suppose no three cricketers who went on to great things in the game have ever come from such a small speck of land. One other Walcott, Leslie, has played Test cricket: once against England in 1929. Leslie, no relation, was ninety years old when he died in 1984. This is nothing unusual: the average life expectancy on the island is eighty-eight, the fifth highest in the world according to United Nations figures.

A total of 77 out of the 221 cricketers who have represented the West Indies were born in Barbados which must make it the most prolific breeding ground for cricketers in the world. It is 166 square miles, 19 square miles bigger than the Isle of Wight, and has a population of around 260,000, many of whom have an affinity with cricket. The sport was brought to the island by the early sugar planters who carved out spaces of flat land to stage their matches. The first ship to arrive from England came early in the seventeenth century but there is no record of its cargo including the island's first cricket bat and stumps. They probably arrived a century later when the game, played in the grounds of country houses and village greens, was taking off in England. Incidentally, in those days there was a lot of gambling on results and gambling has suddenly become one of the issues of the current game.

Just why has Barbados produced so many cricketers of note? I am often asked that question and there are many reasons. There is the climate: the average temperature is around 85–88 degrees with little variation throughout the year and there is sufficient rain to make the soil fertile enough to produce more than sixty thousand tonnes of sugar each year. The soil is well suited to preparing cricket pitches, which roll out flat and easy paced, conditions that suit batsmen. The compact soil binds well together. Cricket is played in the rainy season in Barbados because the planters decided that the sugar cane had to be cut during the dry summer months.

The equable climate makes it possible to play the game without becoming too tired. The humidity level is low because of the trade winds and, providing your head is protected against the sun, a day in the field is not particularly exhausting. Cricket's slow pace suits the West Indian. He is not renowned as a fast mover. When a pedestrian light goes green for him, he is not usually the first man across. People tend to move faster in colder countries.

Cricket also suits the temperament of the Bajans. They are excited when they see a batsman play a stirring shot or a fast bowler knock down the stumps. Then there is beach cricket. Barbados has scores of sandy beaches which are suitable for this type of cricket: a tennis ball is used and the stumps are set in the wet sand. The faster the bowler bowls, or, as often happens, throws, the faster it comes off the sand, which helps the batsman's reactions and his footwork. If the ball is short and bounces high, most will hook it into the sea as far as possible. This is where the average West Indian learns to hook the ball. My family would play beach cricket most Sundays, and when we moved home to a larger property at Black Rock we were closer to the sea; Paradise Beach was our regular rendezvous.

The rule then, as it is now, was that beaches were open to everyone, whatever his colour. There was a beach club near by and the owners tried to keep us off it. We retaliated by running up and down, making exhibitions of ourselves. Most of the businesses then were owned by people of white descent or rich black people and there was some resentment among the other blacks. I believe that this situation influenced the views of Frank Worrell, who was a bit of a rebel and an activist.

When we were not playing cricket or football we went to the cinema. Keith and I loved the Hollywood musicals and spectaculars of the time and often we had to queue up to get in because the films were so popular. The rule for boys was that if you were wearing short pants you were admitted at half-price. Those with long pants paid the full price, and that might explain why, despite being well above average height, I carried on wearing short pants beyond the normal time.

There was rarely time for reading books and our mother was constantly admonishing us about this omission in our lives. One day I was given a copy of a book about Don Bradman, and both Keith and I read it from beginning to end. Our mother was overjoyed. 'They're reading a book,' she said to the assembled family. We spent far more time debating and arguing than we did reading. When it was dark and supper was finished the uncles and aunts would join us to talk about the issues of the day, the state of West Indian cricket, the latest political crisis or whatever took our fancy. We learned a lot from these discussions. Sometimes the exchanges became heated but it was a way of learning about people and events. That is the West Indian way. We love talking.

My Uncle Ernest was a dentist and wanted me to follow him into the profession. I told him I was going to become a cricketer. I was not interested in anything else. I had failed every exam and was to leave school without any certificates. I knew that this was a source of worry for my parents. Harrison College, which I joined at eleven after leaving Combermere, was a fee-paying school.

Keith was two years ahead of me and his sporting feats helped to spur me on. He was a champion sprinter at school and an outstanding footballer, representing Barbados at centre-forward. I also went on to play football for Barbados, I was a full-back. I participated in athletics, too, and specialized in the long jump, hurdles and the high jump; I once won a throwing-the-cricket-ball competition, hurling it more than 121 yards. I was Victor Ludorum in two successive years at Harrison College and still have the plaques today.

My early sporting prowess enabled me to be excused PT and other irksome duties. I wouldn't say I was naughty but I was a little irresponsible at times and liked to enjoy myself. Keith was more serious. He was a much more powerful batsman than me in that period. I was still growing and tended to push the ball rather than hit it. Only when I grew taller, exceeding six feet, did the power come into my batting. I was still known by the name 'Baby' because I was the younger of the Walcott sons.

We also played tennis and table tennis. Our family was middle class by the standards of the day and we had our own table. When we moved house to Black Rock we had a bigger area of land next to the building in which to play our cricket and more of our friends were able to join in.

On Friday nights, after cricket practice, we used to pray that there would be no rain the next day to hold up our match. There were few distractions to take our minds off the major event of the week: the cricket match. No American sports, no television, no videos and no computers. Soon I was working my way up from the third team to the first team, scoring my first century at the age of fourteen.

I had the example of Keith to follow. Between 1937 and 1942 he was one of the most dynamic schoolboy batsmen ever produced by Barbados. I had already made my first-team debut in the Barbados Cricket Association competition for Combermere

School at the age of eleven, making me the youngest player to appear in BCA first-team cricket. It was at Combermere where I first played in the same side as Frank Worrell, who was then a slow left-arm bowler and number ten batsman. Then, as now, the leading schools in Barbados took part in First Division matches with the senior clubs and I believe this is one of the reasons why we produce so many outstanding cricketers. If these youngsters have the ability they rise quickly up the ladder. Today there is more emphasis on scholastic excellence and fewer cricketers of quality are emerging.

Cricket continued to be played during the Second World War but the shortages of food and goods meant a change in habits. The volume of imported food was reduced to a minimum and we had to use our ingenuity. With many young men joining the British forces, jobs were being filled by women and it was noticeable that more blacks were taking the jobs of Englishmen who had returned home.

The only sign of battle in Barbados was the sinking by a German U-boat of the HMS *Cornwallis* in Bridgetown Harbour. The U-boat had pierced the net at the entrance to the harbour. One wartime casualty, though not in that sinking, was the father of Gary Sobers, who was drowned after his ship was torpedoed.

Life went on, practising cricket most evenings, playing on Saturdays, dancing on Saturday nights – I had a liking for the jitterbug, as did Everton Weekes and Frank Worrell. There was an amusing incident in a match between Harrison College and Empire, a leading black club side that featured some of the fastest bowlers on the island, including Manny Martindale, 'Foffie' Williams and Francis Spooner. In the BCA the clubs were run mainly on racial lines. Most had only black players, but there were still some all-white clubs.

In this particular match Herman Griffith, the fast bowler who played for the West Indies in 1933, was captain and his son

Harold was captain of the school team. Herman once bowled Don Bradman for a duck but was not very fast at that time. I was in the sixties and with seven wickets in hand we only needed a dozen or so to win. Herman decided to appeal against the light although I could see little wrong with it. Harold said: 'You can't appeal.' Herman replied, 'Yes you can, but if you want to play at this level, you must abide by the rules.' The umpires gave light and the game ended in a draw. How tough can you be against your son! But he was always known as a very tough man, once sending a fielder off the field for sulking.

One day Keith, who was Harrison College captain, told me the regular wicketkeeper was injured and, knowing that I had kept before, asked me if I was interested in taking over. I told the master in charge of cricket that I would be keen to undertake the role. I had not been scoring too many runs and, although I also did a good deal of bowling, I saw it as a way of cementing my place in the side. That was the start of my wicketkeeping career.

I made three centuries in the 1941–2 season and was chosen for the Barbados trials. That led to my selection for Barbados, who were clearly favouring youngsters at that time. I was one of three schoolboys in the side when I made my debut against Trinidad at Port of Spain on my sixteenth birthday, becoming the youngest player ever to be chosen. Keith had already made his debut at the age of seventeen years, 350 days. My record was to be overtaken four years later when the late Roy Marshall made his debut at the age of fifteen years, 246 days. Roy was a nice man and a fine striker of the ball. He played for Hampshire in county cricket for many years and was very popular with English crowds, performing better in England than he did in the West Indies. His four Test appearances could well have been more because he was undoubtedly Test class.

I had never played on matting before and was extremely nervous in front of around ten thousand noisy Trinidadians, the biggest crowd I had seen up to then. I played and missed a few times and still remember my first run, an edge past gully for three. When I reached a tentative 8 Lance Pierre bowled me with his yorker. I lunged towards mid-off and missed his slower ball. Three years later Everton Weekes made exactly the same score, 8, on the same ground and was dismissed by the same bowler.

We stayed in an old wooden hotel, the Hotel de Paris, and I cannot remember if there were any celebrations of my birthday. Probably not. We were all so young and I did not drink in those days.

I missed the second game against Trinidad because of tonsillitis, which was just as well because I would probably have been dropped if I had not been ill. Opener wasn't really my position. When the two sides met again at the Kensington Oval later that same year I accumulated scores of 70, 67 and 50 and kept my place in the side for the next twelve years until I emigrated to British Guiana and transferred my allegiance to them. By 1944 I had replaced Stanton Gittens behind the stumps and played as the island keeper until 1950.

One of my best innings for Barbados while at school was a patient innings of 125 against British Guiana when I was about to leave Harrison College at the age of eighteen. I captained the school in succession to Keith in my final two years.

When I left school I played for Spartan, Keith's club, and it was an honour when a new pavilion at the club was named after us recently. Both of us captained Spartan and we also represented the club at football.

I had to get a job and that might have proved difficult with no qualifications. However, I obtained a post in the Control Office, a government body that supervised the rationing of food and petrol and fixed prices. It was not the job I would have chosen ... it was difficult to get time off to play cricket.

Just after my twentieth birthday I scored an unbeaten 314

against Trinidad, the highest score by a West Indian up to that point. Jeff Stollmeyer was soon to beat it, though, scoring 324 against British Guiana in 1947. Frank Worrell was my partner for much of that innings and our stand of 574 for the fourth wicket was a world record for a time. It was surpassed by the Indians Vijay Hazare and Gul Mahomed who scored 577 in 1946–7 for Indian state side Holkar against Baroda.

Our stand was just one of many highlights of a memorable and enjoyable career that culminated in me becoming chairman of the International Cricket Council, just about the highest administrative role in the game. Cricket has taken me a long way ... from a backyard near the Kensington Oval to Lord's, the headquarters of the game.

I became the second of the Three Ws to be knighted on Independence Day, 1993. Dame Nita Barrow, the governor-general of Barbados and sister of the late premier Errol Barrow, bestowed the highest honour of Barbados on me, a Knight of St Andrew, at Government House and it was a proud moment for me and my family. I could have gone to London to accept the award from Her Majesty the Queen but decided I would stay at home to receive it.

The Barbados government would have made the recommendation to Her Majesty. Barbados also has its own Honours List, and I have the GCM, the Gold Crown of Merit, for my contribution to cricket administration in the Caribbean, awarded in 1991, and the OBE from the British government, which I received in 1966. When I left Guyana I was presented with the Golden Arrow of Achievement for my contribution to cricket in that country.

'Does it make any difference to your life, being a sir,' I was once asked. It certainly does. People tend to treat me with more respect and it helps open a few doors. I find most people in the Caribbean are unfamiliar with the right usage, often calling me

'Sir Walcott' and Lady Walcott 'Mrs Walcott'. I was coming out of a shopping mall the other day when a man smiled at me and said, 'Hello, Sir Frank.' I replied, 'Frank is dead. I am Sir Clyde!'

There are now five cricketing knights in the history of Bajan cricket: the Three Ws, Sir Garfield Sobers and the latest, Sir Conrad Hunte. Conrad's honour, announced on Independence Day, 30 November 1998, was rightly acclaimed everywhere in the Caribbean. He has been a great ambassador around the world for the West Indies. One of our finest opening batsmen, he played for the West Indies between 1957 and 1967, scoring a century on his debut, and was vice-captain for five years under Sir Garfield Sobers. Injury forced him to retire in 1967 and he became involved in community work in England. After working in financial marketing services and investment in Atlanta, Georgia, he was national development coach for the United Cricket Board of South Africa, doing valuable work in the townships. He is a director of Moral Rearmament and is now back working in his native Barbados.

Further recognition of my work came when I was included on a list of twenty-five distinguished Caribbean sportsmen issued by CARICOM. I received a plaque as a memento. In all my years working in cricket administration I was never paid, and with more money coming into cricket worldwide the role of the amateur administrator may slowly be changing as the game becomes more professional. I believe there has to be a balance between those ex-cricketers like myself who want to serve in order to put something back into the game and those without a cricketing background who join the various boards to offer their financial and commercial expertise. It would not be a good thing to have a board comprised of all commercial people and no ex-cricketers. Nor would it be advantageous to have one full of ex-cricketers, some of whom might have limited business experience. Cricket is fortunate that it has so many of its former players willing to act as administrators. The game needs that to continue. There are far more ex-players working on in cricket than there are ex-players in football administration or in many other sports that attract big crowds. That is where cricket has a considerable advantage.

2   *The Three Ws*

We were like the Three Musketeers, three cricketers from the same part of Barbados, born within eighteen months of each other. We didn't meet until our early teens and we soon became firm friends as we emerged as Test cricketers. We were never rivals; we had too much respect for each other. We all ended up being knighted and the cricket record books have devoted a lot of space to our exploits.

The name 'Three Ws' was coined by an English journalist on the 1950 tour of England and, like most snappy titles that appeal to headline writers, it stayed with us. Sadly, Frank Worrell, the first of us to be knighted, died in 1967. He did not know he was terminally ill until about six weeks before he died in the University Hospital at Mona, Jamaica. A doctor told him, 'It could be six years, or six weeks.' It was the latter. Frank Worrell now lies buried at the University of the West Indies in Barbados along with his wife Velda and his daughter Lana. My son Michael, who played one match for Barbados, was married to Lana at the time of her death.

Frank was the eldest of the Three Ws. He was born on 1 August 1924. Everton Weekes was born on 26 February 1925 and I was born on 17 January 1926. Frank was brought up at Bank Hall, a few hundred yards from the Barbados Test match ground at Kensington Oval; I was born on the corner of Baxter's Road and Westbury Road, somewhat closer to Kensington in the other direction; and Everton was born three hundred yards from Kensington at Pickwick Gap.

West Indians like exotic names, and apparently Everton was named that because his father was an Everton F.C. supporter. Bajans follow English football closely and do the English football pools. When Jim Laker once asked him how he got his name and Everton told him, Jim said, 'It was a good thing your father wasn't a West Bromwich Albion supporter!' Everton's middle name is Decourcey and he tells me he does not know how his parents arrived at that one. 'It might have come from the French influence,' he said. 'I think we had relatives in Dominica.'

Frank Worrell's middle names were even more unusual – Mortimore Maglinne. I never discovered their origins. In cricket scorebooks he was always down as F.M.M. Worrell and I am sure most cricket supporters did not know what M.M. stood for.

I am often asked the question, 'Who was the best of the Three Ws?' and it is not easy to answer. Many experts believe Everton was a better all-round batsman than I was and I agree with that assessment because he had a greater range of shots. It is suggested that Frank Worrell might have had an edge over both of us because he was a fine bowler in two styles, a brilliant fielder and an outstanding captain. He captained the West Indies in fifteen Tests, winning nine of them, and led the West Indies in the epic series in Australia in 1960–1 which revived interest in cricket there following the retirement of Don Bradman. That was the series which featured the first tied Test in history, at Brisbane.

As a batsman, Frank was all elegance and style. He stroked the ball just hard enough to reach the boundary whereas I would drive it with much more power. He appealed more to the connoisseurs. I was involved in many big stands with him, including our world-record fourth-wicket stand of 574 in Port of Spain in 1946, and enjoyed batting with him. His mastery made it easier for whoever was batting with him. He was invariably modest about his achievements, saying after the record stand, 'The conditions were loaded in our favour. I wasn't all that delighted about it.'

I loved batting with Everton, too, and he helped me score quicker because the fielder was always square of the wicket on the offside to try to stop his square cuts, and when I faced I tended to hit the ball straighter. The opposing captain rarely changed the field which made it easier for me to score.

They say figures never lie and when it comes to cricket averages I think that is right. Everton has the best figures of any of us as a batsman: most Test runs with 4455 and an average of 58.61. And he came eighth in the all-time list of West Indian Test batsmen. He played in only forty-eight Tests because there were far fewer international matches in our day. If he had played in 121 like Sir Viv Richards I feel confident he would have surpassed Viv's record total of 8540 runs for the West Indies.

Frank Worrell is twelfth, with 3860 runs, average 49.48, and I am thirteenth, with 3798, average 56.68. I believe I was one of the few cricketers whose first-class average is almost the same (it is 56.64) as my Test average. Everton and I both scored fifteen Test centuries, Frank Worrell nine. Summing up, I think I can say that Everton was the best batsman of the trio, Frank was the best all-rounder (he took sixty-nine Test wickets at 38.73 and forty-three catches) and I was the best wicketkeeper–batsman who bowled a bit, with sixty-four dismissals, fifty-three catches and eleven stumpings, still a West Indian record, and eleven wickets at 37.09. Everton, as he admits, was not a bowler, although he did send down a few overs in Test matches, taking one wicket for 77 runs.

I first played with Frank Worrell when we were at Combermere School together and he was a slow left-arm orthodox bowler and a number ten batsman. He did not stay at ten for long. The house where he was born overlooked the Empire cicket ground and he took an interest in the game almost as soon as he could walk.

His father was in the merchant service and he rarely saw him. His mother, a seamstress, left to live in New York, taking his sister Grace and brother Livingstone with her, leaving Frank to be brought up by his grandmother. Everton believes that Frank was originally a right-handed bowler and only changed after he fell off his bike and broke his right arm. When Frank left the Roebuck Elementary School to join Combermere he came under the influence of Derek Sealy, the master who was the youngest Test player until Mushtaq Mohammed took over from him thirty years later. Sealy encouraged Frank to spin the ball and his games master, V. B. Williams, promoted him from the fourth team to the first team by the age of thirteen. In his first game he went in to bat wearing short pants.

Being promoted so early caused some resentment and his biographer, Ernest Eytle, wrote that he was known as a 'big head'. Eytle also claimed that, though he was well above average as a student, he was not particularly amenable to discipline. He preferred to practise on a corner of the Empire ground, where the groundsman, John Morgan, had prepared a pitch for him and his friends, to organized practice at school.

He was up before the headmaster on a number of occasions. Once he was reprimanded for batting on to score a double century in a house match. The house master was livid, saying, 'Why don't you get out and give someone else a chance to bat?' On another occasion, he was suspended for leaving a match before the end to go to the cinema.

Frank and his friends had a team called the Starvation Eleven and they played cricket every day in the holidays, each match lasting many days. That is where he learned to play long innings. As he said, 'If we weren't in the churchyard playing cricket we were on the beach. Our lives revolved around cricket.'

Cheerful and popular with his team-mates, he developed at that early age a habit that was to stay with him for the rest of his career: at any time he could lie down and take a nap. I can remember someone going up to him, shaking him, and saying, 'You're in, Frank!' He played football for Barbados, like Everton and myself, and also liked playing table tennis and tennis and enjoyed swimming.

After our matches at school, we played together in Barbados trials and then in matches for the island. It was not long before his batting had developed to such an extent that he had moved up to number four in the order and was a fully accredited batsman. But he never lost interest in his bowling. As he became more experienced, he developed the art of seam bowling and later became the first West Indian to open both batting and bowling in a Test match.

There was a wonderful spirit among these young players. We were so dedicated to our cricket that we vowed we would not drink alcohol and instead spent our spare hours playing cards. But Frank did not observe the ban on alcohol. He liked a drink and he liked relaxing. When he skippered the West Indies in Australia in 1961 he banned his players from playing cards, saying, 'I feel it is better for a player to go out and get "bombed", providing he returns to the hotel by twelve o'clock to sleep it off, than for a player to sit up until midnight burning up mental and physical energy at cards. What is more, card-playing is seldom far removed from noggin-taking. I have seen these chaps rise from the card tables as if they had spent the evening at a night club or in a hotel bar. I attribute our impressive fielding in Australia to the enforcement of the no-card-playing rule.'

When Frank left Combermere as a pupil he joined the staff and taught general subjects to the juniors before moving to Trinidad to continue his career. Soon he was back working in Barbados as an insurance agent. He was a young man with an opinion of his own and he had strong views about what he saw as discrimination against black players when it came to the selection of sides. This sense of injustice coloured his views on life generally and turned him into a campaigner on behalf of the poor and the disadvantaged.

After our record stand, which saw Frank make 255 while I scored my highest total of 314, he went to live and work in Jamaica, which he left in 1948 to sign as the professional at Radcliffe in the Central Lancashire League at an annual salary of five hundred pounds. He was to remain with them for twelve seasons but I am sure he earned himself a raise! He should have captained the West Indies side long before the offer finally came his way, and I rated him our best ever skipper. He was at his most formidable on the 1960–1 tour of Australia when he kept his promise that the West Indies would play the game according to their traditions, in an attacking manner, irrespective of whether they were winning or losing. He introduced a number of rules. Batsmen were told they had to cross on the pitch, and if they were given out had to leave the crease without dissent. It was a tour when everyone 'walked' on the visiting side. The Australians were so delighted at the way the series was played that they hosted a farewell dinner for the West Indies team at the end of the tour and announced that a new trophy, the Frank Worrell Trophy, would be presented in future for Test series between the two sides. Worrell and his players were given a ticker-tape farewell in Melbourne, something that had never happened before in Australian cricket.

On his return to Jamaica, Frank was appointed a warden of the University of the West Indies, situated in the valley at Mona, just outside Kingston in Jamaica. That was followed by his appointment as a senator by Prime Minister Sir Alexander Bustamente. Such public service was in keeping with the manner in which Frank conducted himself throughout his life. In a Test match against the Indians one of their opening batsmen, Nari Contractor, was struck on the head by Charlie Griffith and his life put in danger. Frank was one of the people who donated blood.

He always liked a joke. I remember on the 1951 tour of Australia we were playing South Australia and he was bowled first ball by Geoff Noblett. Before his next innings, he decided to kit himself out in a brand-new set of clothing in an attempt to change his luck. He went in, took guard, and was promptly bowled first ball again by Noblett. I was the next batsman in and as we crossed, I said jokingly, 'Why is it that I have to face a hat trick every time I follow you?' He was the thirteenth West Indies captain and the 1951 tour was one time when the luck went against him.

I was in Guyana when I heard the dreadful news that he had died. He collapsed on a tour of Indian Universities and was taken to the University Hospital in Jamaica where he died at 9.40 a.m. on 13 March 1967. There was a feeling of disbelief around the whole Caribbean. People couldn't accept it. Here was a man who seemingly had a great future, a hero whose real work was about to begin.

In Barbados we had a two-minute silence. We always have two minutes, not the traditional one minute. When the funeral took place at St Michael's Cathedral thousands crowded into the building and the immediate area. Everton Weekes was one of the pall bearers. I wasn't asked. Frank's burial site at the University of the West Indies is also the last resting place of his wife Velda who died comparatively young of a heart attack and his daughter Lana, who died of cancer. It is impossible to imagine a sadder end to one of the most heroic episodes in the short history of the independent West Indies.

Everton Weekes was born in a wooden house and his father left home when he was eight to work in the Trinidad oil fields. Everton did not see him again until he was nineteen. Like me, he saw his first Test match at Kensington in 1935, although we didn't meet until we were sixteen, playing together in a Barbados trial match. Everton used to help the groundsman prepare the pitch and when his work was finished he stayed on to watch the game. If he went home and returned he had to pay to get in.

His scholastic record was no better than mine but, also like me, he was an all-round sportsman. He never passed an exam, but later took a course in hotel management and was given the opportunity to study in London, which he declined because he was doing so well in cricket. Between 1943 and 1947 he was in the Barbados army, reaching the rank of corporal. He never served abroad, which was just as well for Bajan and West Indian cricket.

Everton was well ahead of Frank and myself in one area, playing cards. A lifelong bridge player, he has represented Barbados at the game of cricket for many years. He played for the Garrison Sports Club and then Empire.

Short and compact, he was quick on his feet and possessed a variety of shots on both sides of the wicket. About the only shot he did not play so much was the sweep, but then it was less in vogue than it is today. And no one played the reverse sweep. That would have been considered far too risky. Everton scored at a quick rate and was always looking to keep the scoreboard moving. He has been compared to Bradman in that respect. He was never an occupier of the crease.

If he was ever hit on the pad he would worry about it. 'How did I make that mistake?' he would ask. We all believed that you had a bat to hit the ball with and the pad was there to protect your leg if you missed it. The use of the pad by batsmen has been a retrograde step, and I do not like to see it. Although the law has been changed so that a batsman can be given out if he pads away a ball pitching outside off stump and does not play a shot, the tactic continues to this day. The use of the pad was started, I believe, by Colin Cowdrey in the 1957 Test at Edgbaston. Fielders have moved closer to the bat because of this development, and I think that this also harms the game.

Everton was never coached and when he did some coaching

after his retirement he always encouraged young players to obey their instincts and hit the ball. He was outstanding at using his feet and coming down the pitch to slower bowlers, an art which is rarely seen in Test matches these days. The most notable exceptions are Sachin Tendulkar, Brian Lara and Mark Waugh.

Everton was a brilliant fielder in almost any position: outstanding in the covers, a safe catcher at slip. Once he made the move to slip he was so good, in the same class as Wally Hammond and Colin Cowdrey, that he stayed there.

In the 1950 tour of England he made a string of double centuries, including 279 in 235 minutes at Trent Bridge, and the great English batsman of Nottingham, George Gunn, who was among the crowd, said, 'I have seen them all since Victor Trumper and including Bradman. I have never seen a more brilliant array of strokes nor heard the ball so sweetly struck.' After Everton's 200 not out against Leicestershire, which included the fastest hundred of the season, in 65 minutes, Frank Worrell admonished him: 'You must not hit the ball so hard,' he said. 'You give the fielders no chance so they don't chase the ball. Hit a little less hard and they will have to run for it. Watch how quickly they tire.' Everton laughed and did not change his approach.

West Indian cricketers tended to retire earlier than Englishmen and Australians, and Everton retired in 1958 at the age of thirty-three. Some might say he was still in his prime and could have carried on. The same might have been said of me, for I retired at the same time, a year younger, to take up a career in business. Frank Worrell went on longer, until he was thirty-nine. He retired from Test cricket after leading the West Indies to a 3–1 victory in the series in England in 1963.

3 *Test Debut*

I made my Test debut four days after my twenty-second birthday in 1948 on my home ground at the Kensington Oval, less than a mile from where I was born. I was chosen after scoring 120 for Barbados against the English tourists.

One of the opening batsmen was injured and, although I was unaccustomed to going in first, I was asked to open with Jeff Stollmeyer. As we were walking out to the wicket he said, 'You know I never take the first ball.' So in my first Test I took the first delivery. The pitch, which was uncovered, was slightly rain affected and the English offspinner Jim Laker, who was also making his debut, came on after only two overs. He turned the ball a yard from the start and I think I did reasonably well to score 8 before he bowled me. In the second innings I doubled my output, scoring 16 before that fine close fielder Jack Ikin caught me off the bowling of Worcestershire's slow left-armer Dick Howorth. Rain saved England from a heavy defeat in that match.

It was a peculiar England side, the first to visit the Caribbean for thirteen years and certainly the weakest ever to be sent out.

The fourteen-man squad was captained by Gubby Allen, who was forty-five. Gubby was also the manager and played little part on the field after pulling a muscle on the ship coming over. He pulled two more muscles when he attempted to play. Harold Butler, the Nottinghamshire fast bowler, went down with malaria, Dennis Brookes was sent home after breaking a finger,

Joe Hardstaff Jnr. tore a hamstring and Ikin missed one of the four Tests, at Trinidad, when he had a carbuncle. Of the fourteen players, only three, Godfrey Evans, Hardstaff and Ikin, had been in the party to Australia the previous year and Ken Cranston, the Lancashire captain, Howorth and Jack Robertson had played just six Tests between them. Leicestershire's Gerald Smithson was a 'Bevin' boy, a young man conscripted to go down the mines, and had to be given special permission from the Ministry of Labour to make the trip. Discipline was tougher then, just after the end of the war, and when Smithson dropped a catch on the boundary, Allen arranged to take him to a ground near by to practise catching high balls.

A far better squad of players had been left at home, including Len Hutton, Bill Edrich, Cyril Washbrook, Norman Yardley, Reg Simpson, Harold Gimblett, Alec Bedser, Doug Wright, Dick Pollard, Eric Hollies and Denis Compton, who was said to be out having a knee operation, although he played fourteen times for Arsenal that season. In those colonial days we had the impression in the West Indies that the English thought they were superior and considered they 'knew it all'. Barbados citizens had only just won the right to vote in 1948 and we were to remain a colony of Britain until 1966. The English had invented cricket and the MCC drew up the Laws and made any changes they felt were necessary.

Tension can still surface between the two Test sides. On the last tour to the West Indies in 1998 Alec Stewart success-fully appealed for a catch off Shivnarine Chanderpaul when the ball had clearly hit the ground. In a one-day game, when Stewart was given out he argued that there were three fielders inside the circle and refused to walk. The umpire had indeed made a mistake, but when you are given out, you should go.

According to my friend Jim Swanton, a regular visitor to

Barbados, the MCC deliberately chose a weak side for this tour because Karl Nunes, the president of the West Indies Board, had pleaded that West Indian cricket was not in a strong state. Swanton wrote in his book *Gubby Allen – Man of Cricket*, 'His appeal struck a ready chord in the MCC Committee and in particular with Plum Warner, Trinidad born and part educated in Barbados, with whom the West Indians in his sentimental moments were always "my countrymen". It was Gubby's view that Plum was hoodwinked by Nunes with the result that too many unproved cricketers were chosen and too many of the best left at home after a hard tour of Australia and New Zealand.' He considered that some of the outstanding players such as Hutton, Compton and Bedser were being saved for the 1948 tour of Don Bradman's Australians.

The Three Ws all played in that series and Everton Weekes and Frank Worrell both made big scores. I was less fortunate, scoring 20 and 2 at Port of Spain, 11 and 31 at Georgetown and 45 at Kingston, by which time I had been demoted to number eight in the order.

It is true to say I was in the side for my wicketkeeping. In four Tests I was responsible for sixteen dismissals, including five stumpings. My eventual tally of eleven stumpings in my Test career as a keeper remains a West Indian record to this day. And I learned with some surprise from the statistics of Keith A. P. Sandford that I was stumped no less than eight times myself in sixty-seven Test dismissals. I think that indicated a willingness to go down the pitch to take on the slow bowlers. Everton Weekes and Frank Worrell always believed in using your feet to the slow men.

A common misconception about West Indian cricket was that Worrell was the first black man to captain the West Indies when he led the side in Australia in 1960–1. The first to perform the role was George Headley in that 1948 series but he was the first to captain on a tour. His selection was borne out of an odd compromise. It was decided he would lead in the first Test and in the last in Jamaica, with Jeff Stollmeyer in charge in Trinidad and John Goddard in British Guiana. But Headley, who was thirty-eight, hurt his back and Goddard took over again in the fourth Test. I had first seen George playing for Jamaica the previous year when he scored 203 after I had 'caught' him on 6. He played the ball extremely late, the mark of a great player. Like Bradman, when he played a shot it went for runs. He rarely hit the ball near a fielder. He was a very convivial man, always giving advice to the younger players. But he was drinking rather heavily and no longer commanded their total respect.

It was the custom on that tour to appoint a liaison officer for the visiting team from the island or territory where the game was being played and when the Test in Trinidad was played a local official was duly appointed. He failed to appear on the first day, and the following day was spotted playing bridge at the Union Club. Gubby Allen found out where he was, approached him and said, 'I believe that you are our liaison officer.' The man looked up and said, 'Oh no, I've resigned. The job was going to be too much for me!'

Allen made a gallant 77 in that Test, which ended in a draw. He broke down after bowling sixteen overs in the first innings, and with Brookes on his way back home and England needing four substitutes on the field at one stage, the MCC agreed to Allen's request for a replacement. They could not guarantee Compton but they did manage to persuade Yorkshire to release Hutton. He played on a sticky dog of a pitch in Georgetown and was top scorer with 31 in England's first-innings total of 111. Frank Worrell had batted beautifully for his unbeaten 131 in our first innings of 297 for eight, the lowest of his six centuries against England. Allen was injured again and batted with a runner. He was nought not out, coming in at number eleven, before we won by seven wickets. My 31 not out was better than it looked against Laker and Howorth in those bowler-friendly conditions.

Hutton followed up with 56 and 60 in the last Test at Kingston. A masterful 141 from Everton Weekes again left Allen's side trailing and we were victorious by ten wickets to take the series 2–0. Gubby Allen knew his cricket and was an outstanding leader and administrator. I remember in 1957 sitting next to him at an MCC dinner when he asked me if I had seen any useful players on a Swanton tour of the Caribbean some time before. 'Yes,' I said, 'Micky Stewart, the Surrey player.' He replied, 'He picks his bat up the wrong way – towards gully.' That typified for me the English approach to cricket. Everything had to be right. In the West Indies we never bother about how a batsman picks his bat up as long as it comes down the right way.

One of Gubby's many meritorious contributions to cricket was to persuade the MCC to alter the lbw law, making it impossible for a bowler to win an lbw decision if the ball pitches outside the leg stump. This change of the law means that bowlers gain much less benefit from bowling into the rough outside the leg stump. Imagine how many more wickets Shane Warne would have taken had the law not been altered!

I got to know Len Hutton later and found him a man with a dry sense of humour. But on that tour it was difficult to get too close to him. He was shy and tended to look at people out of the corner of his eye.

I was lucky that I was able to study at close quarters the work of Godfrey Evans behind the stumps on that tour. He was six years older than me and the best in the world at the time. It is difficult to compare keepers of different generations because the game is always changing, but standing up and standing back I do not believe there was anyone better. He was very popular wherever he went, both with opponents and spectators and always gave the appearance of enjoying what he was doing. He used to stand up to Alec Bedser and, although not genuinely fast, Bedser was pretty lively.

I had a variety of bowlers to keep to in that series and found it a useful learning experience. There were the quicker bowlers such as Hines Johnson, Prior Jones, Esmond Kentish, John Trim and Foffie Williams and the spin of Wilfrid Ferguson and Jeff Stollmeyer.

While we had George Headley, there were a lot of drinkers in the England squad, too, as I found out when I travelled back on the ship with them on my way to the tour in India that folllowed for us. When the bar closed at 11 p.m. they were still drinking, and next morning they needed to take something to clear their heads.

I had scored only 133 runs in seven innings but my wicket-keeping enabled me to earn selection for the tour of India, Pakistan and Sri Lanka, or Ceylon as it was known in those days. And on that tour I was to do rather better.

4 *Taking on the Indians*

I toured India once, in 1948–9, and it was an unforgettable experience. We travelled everywhere by train, which was not pleasurable. The trains were slow, crowded and did not contain restaurant cars. We had to eat at the stations, jumping out when the train stopped, and buying food off the many vendors. It was a dangerous thing to do but I never had stomach trouble. Some of my colleagues did, and it was not pleasant.

The hotels were a disgrace. Some cities had no hotels so we stayed in old army barracks, lacking in comforts or furnishings. One had no bathrooms and we had to get a dobe to bring a bucket to allow us to bathe. Today's generation of cricketers would not tolerate such primitive conditions. I have been back to India on ICC business since that tour and the transformation is staggering. India now has some of the finest, most elegant hotels in the world and most internal travel by cricket sides is by air.

I remember on one occasion we travelled from Delhi to Poona, over forty hours, arrived tired and bedraggled at 7.30 a.m. and went straight to the hotel for a shower and breakfast before going to the ground to begin a match at 11.30. I seem to remember we were out cheaply, one of the few times that happened. The pitches were mainly hard, dry and good for batting, and it was a high-scoring Test series, dominated by Everton Weekes. He set a record of five successive Test centuries and would have made it six but for being run out for 90 in the final Test.

In some parts of this vast country it was punishingly hot. We used bottled water but most of us had stomach problems and occasionally were forced to miss a day's play. Two of the players had chickenpox. I went in at number eight in one of the warm-up matches at the Cricket Club of India in Bombay and was so tired by the time I reached my hundred that when we came in for tea I cried and said I did not want to resume my innings. I was in a state of collapse.

It was the first West Indian tour of India, which had just split into India and Pakistan following the end of the British Raj. I understood that the Indian Board had asked for George Headley to be picked as captain but our selection committee felt he was too old to lead the side and chose John Goddard instead. Goddard had led the West Indies to victories in the Tests in Georgetown and Kingston in the previous series yet, with just four Tests behind him, a top score of 46 not out from 122 runs and just eleven wickets, his experience was limited. Headley broke down in the first Test in Delhi and took no further part in the tour.

The man who could well have been captain, Frank Worrell, declared himself unavailable when the Board rejected his plea to be paid for the tour. The Board refused to negotiate with him and he stayed at home. He went to India the following winter with the Commonwealth XI, a team of professionals from the Lancashire League, and scored 684 runs in the unofficial Tests for an average of 97.71 with two centuries, including a vintage innings of 233 not out at Kanpur.

The West Indies won the inaugural series 1–0, with four matches drawn. We lost just one of the nineteen first-class matches played and won six. I ended with the highest aggregate of runs, 1366, but was overshadowed by the performances of Everton, who achieved the amazing average of 111.28 in the Tests. I scored 452 runs in the series, at an average of 64.57.

My first Test hundred came in the opening Test in Delhi when

I was run out for 152. If the TV replay had been used in those days I think I would have been given in! Gerry Gomez and I established a West Indian fourth-wicket record of 267, which was only to last for just over a year. Weekes and Worrell beat it with 283 against England at Trent Bridge. We amassed 631 in the Delhi Test and followed with 629 for six in the second Test at the Brabourne Stadium in Bombay. At the time the Wankhede Stadium was still to be built and all the Tests were staged at the colonial-style Brabourne, named after an English governor. Today the Brabourne is hardly ever used for big matches. The two grounds are almost side by side.

The West Indies found the opener they were seeking in Allan Rae, a left-hander with a sound temperament and a commendable defence. He scored two centuries and established a profitable partnership with Jeff Stollmeyer that was to last a long time. Allan, a good friend of mine over the years who has contributed tremendously to the development of West Indian cricket, especially as an administrator, was a bit of a theorist. In one game, after he had just been dismissed by Amarnath, he said to Everton as they passed, 'He's doing everything with it! It's moving in and cutting back off the seam.' Everton played a couple of deliveries which did not seem to do too much and at the end of the over came to me to enquire what exactly was happening. 'Just a little in swing, that's all,' I said. Allan always made things appear more dramatic than they were. After another couple of deliveries, Everton proceeded to knock the ball all over the field.

I scored another century, 108, in the third Test at Eden Gardens, Calcutta, after Goddard won a third successive toss. He went on to win all five tosses, the fourth captain to do so. The match was played over the New Year, which signalled the start of the new India. Everton went one better, scoring two centuries, 162 and 101, in the match, which was drawn. The West Indies won the fourth Test in Madras by an innings and 193 runs to take the series, Prior Jones skittling the Indians for 144 in their second innings. We nearly lost in the fifth Test in Bombay. The Indians were 355 for eight at the close, just 6 runs short in an exciting finish.

I thought I had had a successful series. Keeping wicket in those conditions was tiring, and to end the series with 452 runs, the second highest aggregate behind Everton Weekes's 779, was very heartening. Twenty-three centuries were scored by West Indian batsmen on the tour, six by Everton, six by Allan Rae, five by me, two by Stollmeyer and individual ones by George Carew, Robert Christiani and Gerry Gomez.

An advantage that the West Indies had was that the Indians possessed no bowlers of note faster than medium pace. D. G. Phadkar and Lala Amarnath were both fine bowlers but neither was quick. However, in another few years the Indians did possess the best two slow bowlers of that decade in M. H. 'Vinoo' Mankad, the slow left-armer and Subhash Gupte, the legspin and googly bowler.

The tour ended with a two-week visit to what was then Ceylon. That was an enjoyable trip and we beat Ceylon by an innings and 22 runs in the first match and drew the second; I managed to score 125. In all I was responsible for twenty-seven dismissals behind the wicket, including three stumpings. With Christiani and Cliff McWatt both keepers, I was able to hand over the gloves to them on a few occasions and bowl off-cutters. I bowled sixty-three overs at a cost of 130 runs for one wicket.

The only other time I took part in a series against India, in the West Indies in 1953, I had given up wicketkeeping for the national side. I bowled thirty-five overs in the series and captured two wickets for 48 runs. Once again the batsmen dominated on easy-paced pitches against bowling well below the pace of modern fast bowlers. Four Tests were drawn and we won the second at Bridgetown. I made 98 in that match and was given out lbw by my uncle, Harold Walcott. My first Test hundred on home soil was not long delayed. A month later I made 125 in Georgetown before that fine cricketer Vijay Hazare had me lbw. I recorded 457 runs in the series, at an average of 72.57.

Before the Barbados Test Everton Weekes made a peerless 253 out of the Barbados total of 606 for seven and the sixteen-year-old Garfield Sobers took seven wickets. Everton was again the star of the whole series, totalling 716 runs, with three centuries and an average of 102.28. The absent Frank Worrell had decided to concentrate on his degree course in administration at Manchester University.

It was in India in 1948 that I first took up smoking. Everton Weekes smoked and so did a number of the players. There were no health warnings at the time and no one thought the practice was bad for sportsmen. It was considered chic. A lady in Bombay presented me with an expensive cigarette case and I thought it only right that I should use it. I carried on smoking until the late 1980s, when I decided it was time to stop. I had great difficulty in giving it up.

5   One Hot Party

There have been some hot parties after glorious victories by West Indian cricket teams but none hotter than the one that followed our win at Lord's in the 1950 series. It was the first time we had succeeded at cricket's headquarters and it was a symbolic moment in our lives and in the lives of millions of our countrymen. Many of them were arriving in Britain to build new careers in difficult circumstances because colour prejudice still lingered on. Our win by 326 on 29 June was uplifting for them as well as us. At the time I hardly drank but I had plenty that day.

Thousands of our countrymen came racing on to the outfield, singing and dancing, and I can remember the scene clearly. They were singing the game's most famous calypso, 'Cricket, lovely cricket', with its tribute to 'those two friends of mine, Ramadhin and Valentine'. These two remarkable young bowlers had taken eighteen of England's wickets. I cannot remember who wrote the calypso. It was credited to Lord Beginner, a popular Trinidad calypso singer.

We had beaten England, the country that brought cricket to the Caribbean, at their headquarters! We were intoxicated with delight and pleasure even before we reached the dressing room at the top of the long flight of stairs. Bottles of champagne were produced and Allan Rae, who scored 106 in the first innings, and myself, with an unbeaten 168 in the second innings, were invited to take the first sips as the centurions. I was especially pleased that we were able to share this moment together. After we emptied our glasses, we hurled them to the floor to the cheers of our team-mates.

Our skipper, John Goddard, was a big businessman in Barbados and one of his family's enterprises was distilling rum. He brought a crate of 'Goddard's Gold Braid Rum' with him at the start of the tour and it had been bonded. But when it became apparent on the second day that the West Indies were on their way to a historic victory he applied for its release and it duly arrived. As we toasted each other, and particularly Ramadhin and Valentine, we kept repeating we had won at the Mecca of the game we loved.

When we eventually struggled through the throng outside to our coach we made plans for a party back at our hotel and invited some West Indian students who had supported us to join in.

Frank Worrell, who was taking an economics degree at Manchester University, had to be in Manchester later that night and decided to lock himself in his room for a couple of hours before going to the station. Unfortunately, he overslept and missed the train. He spent the night partying with us instead. In those days the team travelled around the country by train. We had first-class tickets and spent most of the time playing cards. But having to pack at the ground, unpack again at the station and unload again at the other end was rather tiresome.

The four Tests were watched by 372,000 people and the receipts of £94,000 meant that the average cost of a ticket was considerably less than it is today when the best tickets at Lord's can cost up to £40. The West Indies took home £30,000. Not that the players received much of it. We were classed as amateurs and received just five pounds a week and that had to pay for meals taken outside the hotel. So if we entertained anyone to dinner, half our allowance would disappear in one evening. However, the Board did pay us a bonus of £150.

The manager, Jack Kidney, was on his third tour of England and was so pleased to be on the winning side, watched by huge crowds, that he used to look around the packed grounds, totting up the numbers. The West Indies were on a percentage of the takings. The editor of *Wisden* wrote, 'It was the batting which drew the crowds. Even on bad pitches they were superior to their opponents and were always a pleasure to watch. The three coloured players from the tiny island of Barbados stood out in a class of their own, scoring 20 centuries between them. For beauty of stroke no one in the history of the game can have excelled Worrell.'

We had no coach, no physio, no doctor, no masseur, but we did have a priest as our assistant manager, the Revd Palmer Barnes, and he administered to our spiritual needs. He was an Englishman who had moved his home to Barbados. Most of us had a fairly strict Christian upbringing but I do not recall him calling us to prayer meetings. We were doing so well, perhaps we thought we did not need them.

One unusual feature of the series was that the West Indies used just one recognized fast bowler in each of the four Tests. Some difference to today when the West Indies rarely take the field without four fast bowlers. Hines Johnson played in two Tests while Prior Jones took over in the other two. That left Gerry Gomez, a medium-pacer to open the bowling in the first Test and Frank Worrell to do the job in the other three. Frank started out as a slow bowler and, like Gary Sobers, was also able to bowl at a fair pace, left arm round the wicket or over, depending on circumstances.

Our match winners, of course, were Ram and Val, who shared 59 of the 77 wickets taken in the Tests and took 258 in all 31 matches played. Their meteoric rise to fame was one of the great romances of cricket. A few weeks before the tour started Sonny Ramadhin was an unknown cricketer in south Trinidad. He was spotted by a cricketer from Barbados, Clarence Skinner, who was impressed by the unorthodox mixture of off spin and leg spin Ram bowled in a club match. None of the batsmen was able to read him.

Ramadhin was known as Sonny but no one knew his real name. He was invited to take part in the Trinidad trials and bowled well enough to be chosen for the two-match inter-island series against Jamaica. Playing in that match was another unknown twenty-year-old: Alf Valentine from Jamaica. Whereas Ramadhin had no coaching of any kind, Valentine was one of the few players in the West Indies squad to have been coached. Jack Mercer, the former Sussex, Glamorgan and Northants player (who died at the age of ninety-two in 1987), coached him on a visit to Jamaica and said later, 'I knew from the first time I saw him that he was going to be a winner. He used to turn up every day on time with a small case which had two balls in it. I told him he should spin the ball more and should not be satisfied until his fingers started to bleed. A few days later he turned up with two fingers looking very red. I don't know where he got the red ink from!' That was Val's secret. He imparted so much spin to the ball and bowled at such a pace, quicker than most slow left-armers, that the best equipped of batsmen had problems with him on the flattest of pitches. When conditions were favourable he could be unplayable.

Ram bowled with his sleeves rolled down in the traditional Indian manner. He was the first East Indian to appear in Test cricket for the West Indies, even though Trinidad has long had a tradition of producing spin bowlers of Indian origin. Indians were transported there by the British and indentured in the late nine-teenth and early twentieth centuries to work in the oil fields and sugar plantations. It proved to be a good source of labour ... and cricketers. Ram was brought up by friends and relatives and his career blossomed after he was persuaded to join the Trinidad Leaseholds Oil Company. Both Ram and Val had played just two first-class matches when they were selected for the tour. The bold choice to include them must rank as the most inspired selectorial decision of all time. The selectors played a hunch and it came off, with Ram taking 26 wickets at 23.23 in the four Tests and 135 wickets in 21 games in total, and Val 33 wickets at 20.42 in Tests and 123 in all at 17.94.

Tall and unassuming, Val wore glasses and was often ribbed about his short-sightedness. He was known to drop a catch or two off his own bowling. Like Ram, he was a very pleasant young man. His control and spin made him the ideal foil for Ram, who was soon labelled a 'mystery bowler' by the English press. We did not discourage this belief. The English batsmen made it harder for themselves by formulating all kinds of theories and the only one who could read him was Glamorgan's Gilbert Parkhouse, who was left out after scoring 69 in the third Test.

I first met Sonny on the ship coming over, and although we had plenty of time to talk we had no opportunity for me to study his bowling methods. That happened only at the start of the tour on a cold day in Eastbourne when we played a friendly against Colonel Steven's XI. I had a long net against him and was still not certain about which way the ball was going until it bounced because he appeared to bowl every delivery with the same action. But the next day I solved the mystery and was never caught out again. As I was the wicketkeeper that was just as well!

One player who had no idea of which way the ball was going was Doug Insole of Essex, later to become one of England's leading administrators and a good friend of mine. Ram had only to bring his arm over for Insole to be in the most dreadful of muddles. Len Hutton could not pick Ram's leg break but, being a great player with a fantastic eye, he played the ball off the wicket.

Unusual bowlers like Ramadhin, Clarrie Grimmett, B. S. Chandrasekhar and, more recently, Shane Warne have been match winners in Tests because they provided something different.

English cricket has suffered in my view because it was rarely able to give an opportunity to a bowler of this type. Doug Wright, the Kent leg-spinner, was one of the few, and he could never be certain of a place in the England side.

I don't recall Ram or Val ever being injured on that tour, despite bowling 1043 and 1185 overs respectively. By today's standards that is an unheard-of number. If they had a niggle, they just got on with it. When he is getting wickets, no bowler feels tired. They bowled some bad balls, particularly Ram, but England's batsmen were in such a state they were not able to take advantage of them; their feet were in the wrong position. The West Indies over rate was phenomenal, more than twenty an hour throughout the day. No one was bothered about over rates in those days. The public just wanted to see exciting cricket and we did our best to provide it.

We were given plenty of advice before we left about how to cope with English conditions. Most of it concerned warm clothing, and we soon found out how necessary an overcoat was in the early English summer. How Worrell and Weekes, who were playing in the Lancashire League, and the other England residents, George Headley and Learie Constantine, survived the winters was a mystery to the rest of us. We did a lot of singing to remind us of home. Lance Pierre had a fine bass voice and played the piano. His rendering of 'Ol' Man River' was a particular favourite. He and Stollmeyer were the calypso experts.

Our one complaint was about food. It was still in short supply in England just five years after the end of the war and we were fed up with the daily grind of roast beef, boiled potatoes and soggy cabbage. One day at a hotel in Leeds we asked the chef for some rice for our meal, as this was our staple diet. At dinner the waiter brought our main course with the usual roast beef, peas and boiled potatoes. We awaited the rice, but it did not appear. The waiter kept saying the rice was coming. Lo and behold the rice eventually came in the form of rice pudding, as dessert. We were somewhat disappointed. We complained to Mr Kidney, and as the funds were coming in he gave us an extra allowance to eat in London at a Chinese restaurant owned by the boxer Freddie Mills.

There was little sign of colour prejudice, although in the smaller towns where there were no coloured inhabitants people tended to stare at us. I had an amusing experience standing outside a hotel in Nottingham when a little old lady came up to me, stared hard at me, and then proceeded to rub her fingers on my hand to see whether the black would come off.

We had to attend far too many official functions. That was the convention in England at the time and the players were soon bored with cocktail-party small talk. At one function we were a little upset when the speaker described the coming series as 'a good chance to try out some of the young English players for the tour of Australia in the winter'. It was hard to avoid the patronizing tone in his voice and such comments helped motivate our players and made them more determined to do well. The tendency in English cricket was to relate everything to the matches against the Australians, as though the other countries were bit-part players.

We had an early setback when the Middlesex leg-spinner Jim Sims took seven wickets for the MCC and we lost heavily. The manager was livid and wouldn't let us leave the dressing room until he told us what he thought of our performance. Some of us had appointments to have our hair cut. They had to wait.

The pitch for the match against Lancashire at Old Trafford was unfit for a first-class match and if it had been a modern county match the home side would have surely been docked twenty-five points, which is now the rule in English cricket. Alf Valentine took thirteen wickets and we won by an innings. The pitch alongside the one we used for the Lancashire game had been set aside for use in the upcoming Test match but looked just as bad.

At the last minute, the ground authorities decided to move to another strip. This one was totally unprepared and had cracks all over it. We thought it would be dangerous to play on it. The West Indies is not the only place in the world where there are problems with pitches!

Over the years I suspect England have had more problems than most countries with their pitches. The list is a long one, Old Trafford in my day, the ridge at Lord's, dust bowls at the Oval. The West Indian authorities were rightly criticized after the first Test in the series against England in 1998 was abandoned on the first morning, but it was pleasing to hear later in the year that Mike Smith, former England and Warwickshire captain, on behalf of the ICC, had visited Sabina Park to watch a match played on the relaid pitch and declared it was back to the standard required for Test cricket.

The West Indies lost by 202 runs in the first Test at Old Trafford in 1950, and there was a strong feeling afterwards that we should have lodged a formal complaint with the MCC. We decided against it and our representatives merely raised the question of substandard pitches at the next meeting of the ICC the following month.

Eric Hollies and the left-arm spinner Bob Berry of Lancashire captured seventeen of our wickets, with Alf Valentine showing in England's first innings that an outstanding new spin bowler had suddenly arrived on the scene. His figures of eight for 104 in fifty overs was the best debut performance by any West Indian bowler.

I do not recall a team meeting afterwards to sort out what went wrong. John Goddard didn't believe in them.

Bailey was unfit for the Lord's Test and was replaced by York-shire slow left-armer Johnny Wardle. This meant that England had three slow bowlers moving the ball away from the right-handers – Wardle, Berry and Roley Jenkins. They were all useful bowlers in their way but it did not constitute a balanced attack. Our first-innings total of 326 was around par and England's reply of 151 well under par. None of Norman Yardley's batsmen could cope with Ram and Val, who shared nine wickets for 114 runs.

When Goddard declared in our second innings I was still there on 168 not out, one short of George Headley's highest individual total by a West Indian in England. It did not bother me. The sounds of calypsos filled Lord's and one line I remember was 'Gomez broke them down while Walcott knocked them around.' There was a West Indian atmosphere in the great old ground. In their second innings Cyril Washbrook, the dogged opening partner of Hutton, was the only Englishman to hold up Ram and Val with a solid 114. Our two twenty-year-olds managed to share another nine wickets and our margin of victory was 326 runs.

The third Test at Trent Bridge, a ten-wicket win for the West Indies, was notable for one of the most graceful innings ever played at this intimate Test ground – Frank Worrell's 261, the highest total by a West Indian in England. In all, the West Indies set seven records. Whereas I specialized in powering the ball past fielders, Frank would glide it through them with perfect timing and style. Sir Pelham Warner, the former England captain who went to school at Harrison College, Barbados, said the batting of Worrell and of Weekes, who was not far behind with a beautiful innings of 129, was 'the best I have seen in my whole career of playing and watching'. Once again Washbrook recorded a century as Ram and Val reeled off a record number of overs while taking another eight wickets between them. Val's ninety-eight overs in the second innings for 140 runs was a record.

Cricket lovers saw batting of a different kind at the Oval in the final Test which the West Indies won by an innings and 56 runs to make it 3–1 in the rubber. It came from Len Hutton, and was a masterful display of defensive batting on a pitch that took spin after some overnight rain. Standing close behind him with the gloves on taught me a great deal about technique in such conditions. When Len played a defensive shot the ball dropped no more than a yard away, his relaxed grip on the handle making sure there was no chance of a catch being offered to a close fielder. In the tense atmosphere of Test cricket it is not easy to play like that. Hutton had immense powers of concentration. His approach was just as impressive when the odd bad ball came along. He picked the gaps to stroke it for four. There are those who claim that Hutton's unbeaten 202 out of his side's 344 was a selfish innings. That was unfair: when he was on 199 he turned down a chance to take a single several times to keep last man Doug Wright from the bowling. We did believe, however, that he was lucky to survive an lbw appeal from Val and a 'catch' by Christiani at leg slip. Compton, too, was fortunate to be given the benefit of the doubt against a ball from Ram that was slightly quicker and beat his defensive stroke to strike the pad. Compton was run out and was not happy about it. His stand with Hutton was worth 109 when Hutton turned a delivery to fine leg and Compton called for a run. Hutton started to come, changed his mind, and returned to his crease, leaving Compton stranded. Hutton went in again straight away after the last man fell in England's first innings and promptly fell to Goddard, bowling medium-paced off-cutters.

There are many traditionalists who would welcome a return to uncovered pitches. It would make the game more interesting and help batsmen improve their technique, the argument goes. That is all very well in England where wet, drying pitches are rarely dangerous. In the Caribbean, Australia, India and Pakistan, wet pitches are usually unplayable once the hot sun comes out, and for that reason the ICC has had to standardize playing conditions.

Half the population of Barbados seemed to be on the quayside when our ship returned home from England. The harbour was bedecked with flags and the governor was there to meet us, along with other dignitaries. Hundreds of people had clambered up the masts of yachts and schooners. Steel bands played. It was a memorable day, especially for the Three Ws.

Before I left for England I was working in insurance on a commission basis, which was a precarious way of earning a living for someone who was about to marry. During the tour I received an offer of nine hundred pounds a year to play for the Lancashire League side Enfield. I spoke to Everton and Frank, who were both playing in the Lancashire League, and they told me Enfield was one of the least successful clubs. They still advised me to take the offer and I accepted their advice. My parents were not keen on the idea of me being away so long again but soon agreed it was the right course for me.

6   *Happy Days at Enfield*

One of the happiest periods of my career was between 1951 and 1954 when I played as the professional at Enfield. It was not possible for West Indians to play county cricket at the time. That did not happen until 1968 when the regulations were changed to allow counties to field an overseas player. The only way for a West Indian player to make some money abroad was to play in the Leagues and many of us took the opportunity. Some still do.

Muriel and I had just got married and she came with me. It was her first visit to England and, like me, she found it difficult to acclimatize to the weather. Heavy sweaters and overcoats were a priority in the early weeks of the season and a raincoat and umbrella were always close at hand. We lived in digs with a widow we knew as Auntie Belle, across the road from the ground. We paid her three pounds a week and Muriel cooked our meals, usually the West Indian variety.

Enfield is in a small town called Clayton-le-Moors and everyone knows everyone else. There was no telephone in the house and every time we had to make a call we would walk to the telephone kiosk at the end of the road. The locals would say, 'The pro has used the phone this morning' or 'The pro was at the bank.' It was such a friendly place that we soon made many friends. Indeed, we still have friends from our days there. The time went by quickly. There was practice four nights a week and on Saturday nights we went dancing or to the cinema.

I was the first professional at Enfield to arrive with a good Test record and when I left in 1954 I was followed by a succession of other West Indians, including Nyron Asgarali from Trinidad, Conrad Hunte, whose aggregate of 1437 runs in 1959 set a record, Charlie Stayers and Keith Barker. Enfield had not won the League since 1909 and was just as unsuccessful in the Worsley Cup. I knew it would be an impossibility to turn that round. We simply did not have enough good players. But by the time I left we finished runners-up to Todmorden which was a source of pleasure to everyone connected with the club.

Everton Weekes had joined nearby Bacup in 1949. In that year Cec Pepper, the Australian all-rounder, and Vijay Hazare, the Indian all-rounder, both performed the double in the Lancashire League. Pepper was an amazing character. He hardly ever stopped talking and his language was . . . well, very peppery and expressive. His record in 1949, his first season in the League, was 1070 runs and 113 wickets. For some reason he never played Test cricket. After his spell with Burnley he became a first-class umpire. Pepper's usual greeting to Indians and Pakistanis was, 'Have you brought your prayer mat wth you, because you will f—ing need it.'

Dave Edmundson, the current cricket secretary of Lancashire, recalls in his book *See the Conquering Hero: The Story of the Lancashire League* that Pepper used to bowl a bewildering mixture of leg spin, topspin, googlies and flippers, and even his subcontinent opponents, used to that type of bowling in their own countries, were left bamboozled by it. He would stand at the crease, hands on hips, and say, 'As a batsman you would make a f—ing good snake charmer!' or 'Your bat has more edges than a threepenny bit.' After they won the title in 1950 the Burnley club found themselves in trouble when Pepper made some strong comments to the then president of the League. The matter was only resolved when a written apology was handed over.

Another Australian all-rounder with a similar personality was Bill Alley, who later played for Somerset. Bill was the first batsman to score more than 1000 runs in five successive seasons, when he played for Colne. He was a good medium-paced bowler as well, as he showed in county cricket with Somerset. He never stopped talking either and, like Pepper, became a respected umpire.

Leg-spinners abounded in those days in the Lancashire League. Bruce Dooland played for East Lancs with Colin McCool following him there for two seasons. The Indian whom I rated as one of the best leg-spinners of all time, Subhash 'Fergie' Gupte, was at Rishton between 1954 and 1957. Gupte was a great spinner of the ball and, on pitches not up to Test standard, was sometimes unplayable.

'Collie' Smith was another West Indian to set records in the Lancashire League, his score of 306 not out for Burnley in the Worsley Cup in 1959 helping the club to a record total of 523 for nine. He was credited with the longest hit at the ground, the ball landing more than 130 yards away in the middle of an adjoining football field. Burnley was a leading football club at the time but they loved their cricket, too, and the whole town was plunged into mourning on 7 September 1959 when the news came through from the hospital in Stoke-on-Trent where Collie had been taken following his car crash that he had died from his injuries. The vehicle he had been travelling in had collided head on with a cattle wagon on a single-lane road near Stoke. Also in the car were Gary Sobers, at that stage the professional at Radcliffe, who was driving, and Tom Dewdney, the professional at Darwen. Three of Collie's closest cricketing friends, Frank Worrell, Sonny Ramadhin and Cec Pepper were at his bedside when he died. Fortunately, Sobers and Dewdney only sustained minor injuries.

The local newspaper writer, Alf Thornton, wrote of Collie: 'He had it in him to become the next Constantine of the Lancashire

League.' Learie Constantine had nine seasons as Nelson's professional between 1929 and 1937 and in that time they won the title seven times. He took 776 wickets and scored 6363 runs. He lived in Nelson for twenty years, and when he was given a peerage he was made Lord Constantine of Nelson and Maraval, the latter being his place of birth in Trinidad.

The list of West Indians who played in the Lancashire Leagues includes many Test players, including George Headley, Frank Worrell, Everton Weekes, Sonny Ramadhin, Manny Martindale, Basil Butcher, J. K. Holt, Roy Marshall, Ellis Achong, Lance Gibbs, Charlie Griffith, Wes Hall, Clive Lloyd, Seymour Nurse, Michael Holding, Viv Richards, Keith Arthurton and Roger Harper.

The rules were strict, and when Everton Weekes, then at Bacup, took time off in 1951 to play in a game at Brighton, he was suspended. Professionals were not supposed to play in other matches except for designated charity games. There was almost a revolt in Bacup and one player climbed the roof of the pavilion and daubed in white paint on the slates 'We Want Weekes'. The League eventually withdrew their ban. Frank Worrell was playing at Radcliffe and the three of us with our wives would meet at his house on Fridays and his wife Velda would cook a real West Indian meal.

Muriel and I became close friends of the Simmons family in Clayton-le-Moors, who lived close to the Enfield ground. The grandfather and father of the family had played for Enfield and the son was Jack, who would go on to be a long-serving Lancashire all-rounder and who is now chairman of Lancashire County Cricket Club. We spent many happy hours with them, and Jack blames me for his penchant for fish and chips.

On Sundays we used to travel together by coach to play charity matches all over the North. These matches were arranged by Bruce Pairaudeau, the West Indian Test player who was studying in England. We had a very powerful side and never lost.

Just after the war the total attendance at Lancashire League matches was seven hundred thousand a year, and gates were still comparatively high, around two to three thousand a game depending on the names of the two competing professionals. The admission charge was one shilling and three pence.

The art of good living for the professional was to ensure that he always had a collection to supplement his wages. Pepper was the outstanding performer when it came to collections, making sure that he reached his fifty, then maybe his hundred, at just the right time. Any batsman approaching these landmarks had to ensure he did not get there too quickly in the final moments. It was better to get to 48 or 49 and play out a few balls without scoring to give the collectors time to organize themselves. On a good day the professional could pick up twenty pounds from a collection. I used the money to go on trips to places like Blackpool in the car I had bought. Muriel and I liked going to the shows on the Golden Mile and at Morecambe.

I had my best season with the bat at Enfield in 1951, scoring 1136 runs at an average of 71. I made 19 runs fewer in 1953 but finished that season with an average of 111.54. In four seasons I totalled 3991 runs, at an average of 75.30, and took 221 wickets, average 13.39.

At the end of the 1951 season I was selected for the tour of Australia that winter and stayed on in England before travelling by boat with the other players while Muriel went home to give birth to our son Michael. Nine months elapsed before I was able to return home to see my son. That was how it was in those days. Nowadays touring sides will let their players go home during a tour to be present at the birth. This happened on England's last tour to Australia when Lancashire wicketkeeper Warren Hegg was given special dispensation to fly home. In my playing days, even if I had been given permission, I wouldn't have been able to afford it.

7 An Ill-disciplined Tour

Len Hutton's tour of the West Indies in 1953–4 was, in my opinion, even stormier than the Bodyline Tour of Australia in 1932–3. If the present system of disciplining players by referees under the ICC's code of conduct had been in use in those days, I believe half of Hutton's players would have been fined or suspended.

The general view at the time was that the MCC party that arrived in Jamaica just before Christmas was the most unpopular ever to tour the Caribbean. It was a tour full of controversies. There was the bottle-throwing incident in British Guiana, the no-balling of Tony Lock for throwing, and the behaviour on and off the field of many other England players. I exempt the home side of any blame. West Indian cricketers have never been ones to initiate sledging, but I have to admit that, if they are sledged, they react.

The reputation for sportsmanship of previous English touring sides lay in tatters by the end of the tour. There were far too many contested umpiring decisions and word soon spread around the Caribbean that Hutton's side lacked the sportsmanship normally associated with English cricket.

The series was billed as the unofficial championship of the world, England having recently beaten Australia in England to regain the Ashes. But it was ruined for many because Hutton allowed some of the fieriest characters in his side to offend against both the Laws and the spirit of the Laws. Some of the language directed against our players was appalling and would not be tolerated today.

The Laws clearly state that the captain is responsible for ensuring that play is conducted within the spirit of the game and I am afraid Len Hutton, England's first professional captain, had much to answer for on that tour. He was a fine tactician but a captain needs more than that to succeed. He must be a good disciplinarian and a leader of men.

With some questionable players in the England side it was essential that the manager should be a strong character. Although Charles Palmer was a well-respected and pleasant man, in many ways he did not give the impression of having a strong personality. The task of leading the side and helping out the manager proved too much for Hutton, who was thirty-seven and showing signs of tiredness. His players were allowed to get away with far too much and I can confidently say that if a West Indies touring side had behaved in the same way, then they would have run the risk of being sent home. And those concerned would certainly have been in trouble with their Board.

There were umpiring mistakes, no one disputed that, but there has never been a match played at Test level where every player was satisfied with every decision. If there are injustices, they usually cancel each other out. Players have to accept that the umpire's word is final.

Right from the start of the tour Hutton's party was unhappy. They complained that their hotel in Jamaica for the first Test had been too noisy. Dogs had kept the players awake, apparently. That may have been so but I remember being wakened on a number of occasions while staying at hotels in England by shunting trains. After the game against British Guiana in Georgetown, Palmer asked the West Indies Board if different umpires could be appointed for the third Test which was to follow immediately afterwards. He wanted the umpires for the match to be those employed in the Barbados Test, H. B. 'Cortez' Jordan and my uncle, Harold Walcott. Personally, I would have been very happy to have my uncle in charge, although he had once given me out when I felt he had made a mistake. I never talked to him about that. The West Indies Board rejected the request from the England camp as it was against their normal policy and they did not want to pay the expenses of transporting the two officials from Barbados. They were very short of money then, as they are now.

When the locals heard that the England team was asking for the umpires to be replaced they were naturally not too happy about it. Two more officials were appointed, one of them the groundsman 'Badge' Menzies, and they promptly found themselves innocent victims when the crowd started throwing bottles on to the outfield after the local player Cliff McWatt had been given run out, quite rightly, for 54.

I have no doubt at all that the trouble was sparked by someone who had too much to drink reacting when his bet on McWatt to make a big score had come unstuck as a result of the decision. Menzies was involved in two other decisions that would doubtless be referred to the third umpire today. The first was when Robert Christiani, a member of the British Guiana side, was caught low down at midwicket by Willie Watson off Jim Laker. Christiani waited for the umpire to give him out, as he was justified in doing. The next controversy concerned the dismissal of Everton Weekes by Tony Lock. Everton was beaten but did not hear the sound of the wicket being broken and thought it might have been disturbed by Godfrey Evans. Lock admitted he did not have a clear view and the matter was resolved when Evans, as good a sportsman as there has been in international cricket, confirmed that Everton had indeed been bowled. The crowd was not too happy about it, especialy as Everton was on 94.

They were even more irate soon afterwards when McWatt was

run out going for a second run that would have brought up the hundred stand in partnership with J. K. Holt. McWatt realized he was out and returned to the pavilion. His place was taken by the next batsman, Sonny Ramadhin, and it was then that the bottles started coming on from the schoolboys' stand.

Most of the bottle-throwing incidents in West Indian cricket have involved English teams. It was suggested to Hutton by a local official that he ought to take his players off the field until the trouble subsided and the debris had been cleared away. Hutton declined. It was a nasty demonstration and we all agreed that it had been caused by the reaction of one person, probably the worse for drink. I do not think it was aimed at the English players, even though their actions had aroused some antipathy. England won that Test by nine wickets. It was not a good one for either Frank Worrell or myself.

Frank was always on edge about playing in Georgetown, where for some reason he was not as popular as he was at other grounds. He fell twice to that gentleman of bowlers Brian Statham, for nought and 2, after being asked to open when J. K. Holt pulled a muscle. I had scored 220 in our victory two weeks earlier in the second Test in Bridgetown and felt in good form. I did not last long. Statham bowled me for 4 in the first innings and when I went for 26 in the second innings I became Jim Laker's thousandth victim in first-class cricket. Without the benefit of modern replay technology, I have to confess I could not be sure, but at the time I was convinced the ball wouldn't have hit any of the stumps. Jim confirmed that later when he admitted, 'I only asked because it would be my thousandth!'

I struck up an early friendship with Jim. He had the dry sense of humour of a Yorkshireman and we were constantly ribbing each other. He was a great bowler with excellent control, plenty of spin and a good delivery which drifted straight on. I cannot think there has been a better English offbreak bowler in my time, if not all time. Jim got me out thirteen times in first-class cricket, and eleven times in Tests, more than any other bowler. I suppose I had to go down as his bunny, in the same way as Arthur Morris, the Australian batsman, was the bunny of Alec Bedser. When playing Jim, I tended to plant my front foot straight down the pitch, with the bat in front of my pad. This made me more vulnerable to the offbreak or inswing bowler. I never had the same problem with the leg-spinner or outswing bowler.

The English selectors had not made the mistake of their previous disastrous tour six years earlier when some of their best players were left behind. This time the only absentee of note was Alec Bedser, who was unable to come for what was described as business reasons. Bedser never toured the West Indies, which was regrettable because I feel the West Indian cricket lovers would have enjoyed seeing him in action.

I have no hesitation in classing him as a great bowler. At his best he was the same pace as Wasim Akram is today, lively enough to trouble the best of batsmen, particularly when conditions suited him. When he was bowling with the new ball he moved it into the batsman but when the shine wore off he bowled a good leg-cutter. Whenever I have met him since, he has bemoaned the lack of stamina in modern bowlers, constantly reminding people of how long he bowled in a day. He certainly bowled a great many overs and was an amazingly strong man. It must have been something in his genes. I was delighted when I heard that Prime Minister John Major had put Alec's name forward for a knighthood in 1997.

Even the presence of Alec Bedser probably would not have made too much difference to the strength of the England attack in that 1953–4 series, because Hutton had one of England's strongest bowling line-ups at his disposal. The reliable and accurate Brian Statham opened the bowling with Trueman and first change was

Trevor Bailey, one of the outstanding medium-fast bowlers of his or any other era. The spinners were Jim Laker and Tony Lock, and I doubt whether there has been a better pair working together in the history of cricket. Sonny Ramadhin and Alf Valentine may have taken more wickets in the early 1950s and bowled more overs, but on all pitches I would nominate Lock and Laker. Ram and Val were successful on the softer, uncovered pitches of England; less so on the harder pitches of Australia. In two of the Tests a third spinner was used by England, the Yorkshireman Johnny Wardle. He, too, was a fine bowler, with probably more variety than Lock. But Tony was more dangerous; although one of the reasons was that up to that 1953–4 tour he had been allowed to get away with chucking his faster ball. Just why he had not been called to account when bowling with this highly dubious action was a mystery, but he was not the only chucker to escape. Then, as now, I am sure the umpires were instructed to call a bowler if they felt sure his action infringed the Laws. But for some reason umpires have always been reluctant to take this drastic step. The Australian captain Ian Johnson was another bowler with a suspect action, and there were two Australians whom I never saw Ian Meckiff and Gordon Rorke.

Sir Donald Bradman can be credited with having played a leading part in eradicating chucking from Australian cricket. Various English administrators tried to do the same in their country but it was a slow process. Perhaps umpires are reluctant to act because it causes such a fuss, but they must do so for the sake of the game. At umpires' conferences now, we stress that action must be taken in the event of a bowler not conforming to the Laws. Modern technology enables us to have a better idea about the legality of a bowler's action, but the ultimate decision has to be made by the umpire in the middle. After the Sri Lankan offspinner Muttiah Muralitharan was filmed and his action was reviewed it was said that he had been 'cleared' by the ICC. No one is ever cleared. If they were they would be given a licence to turn up at their next match and throw! What we say it that a particular action has been assessed on the basis of the evidence and it appears to be a legal one. That was the case with Muralitharan, only for him to be no-balled again in Sri Lanka's tour of Australia in 1999.

In the West Indies' second innings of the first Test at Jamaica, George Headley, recalled to the side at the age of forty-four after a run of good scores, was bowled by a fast delivery from Lock that was the most blatant throw I have ever seen. Neither umpire saw anything wrong with it and Headley had to go. It was a sad end to an illustrious career that would no doubt have been even more successful had the war not intervened.

The turning point in Lock's career came in the Barbados v. MCC match which preceded the second Test. My Uncle Harold was one of the umpires and when Lock tried his faster ball to Garfield Sobers he called 'no ball' from square leg. Unfortunately, Harold was a little late on the call and the MCC players thought he had called after the ball had bowled Sobers. They protested but, of course, were overruled. Lock was called several more times, by both umpires, and this match signalled the end of his use of the faster ball. My view at the time was that Lock certainly threw his quicker delivery and there were many other deliveries that infringed the Laws. When I toured England in 1957 I was surprised to discover that, although slower in pace, he still bowled the occasional suspect delivery. Lock was shown a film of his bowling and was so shocked by it that he vowed to change his action. He did so and was never as effective again. His remodelled action limited the turn he could put on the ball and he was much less of a threat, although he did go on and play forty-nine Tests, the last of them at the age of thirty-eight and his 174 wickets at 25.58 made him England's tenth most successful Test bowler, only nineteen wickets behind his great partner Jim Laker. I always got on well with him. He was a lively, aggressive competitor and a brilliant fielder in a number of positions. His speciality was short leg or leg slip and he held some magnificent catches close on the legside.

He dismissed me for a duck in that MCC match against Barbados but in the second Test I made 220, the highest innings of my Test career. I came in at 11 for two after Stollmeyer and Worrell had fallen for ducks. I felt in good form. The bat that I had used for the duck was replaced by a new one and I told Lock when we were both in the middle: 'I am going to give you some stick.' Hutton tried to slow me down, setting deep-set fields to restrict me to singles. I enjoyed the battle and it was particularly satisfying to record my highest total on my home ground.

The West Indies won that Test by 181 runs, 41 more than they had won the first Test by in Jamaica. Jeff Stollmeyer, the West Indies captain, had declared in the opening Test, setting England 457 to win in nine hours. Watson scored 109, putting on 130 with Hutton, who made 56, and with Peter May contributing a stylish 69 England still had a chance of victory. May, in my view the supreme English batsman of his generation, was well on course for a century when he was the victim of one of the many poor umpiring decisions in the series. Worried about the way May was forcing the pace, Stollmeyer asked opening bowler Esmond Kentish to try some leg theory, bowling down the legside to slow things down. England could hardly complain at the tactic. They had used it themselves on a few occasions, notably in a home Test match against the Australians in 1948 when Trevor Bailey was given the task. May, trying to force a delivery a foot or so outside the leg stump, found himself being given out, caught by wicketkeeper McWatt. I was fielding at first slip and did not appeal. I thought the ball had come off May's pad.

Kentish went on to take five wickets and the West Indies won by 140 runs. Hutton had made the mistake of packing his side with quick bowlers: Statham. Trueman, Bailey and Alan Moss, who was making his Test debut. But the pitch was much slower than the one normally found at Sabina Park. Denis Compton had to be used as a spin bowler, and although he was capable of bowling the occasional Chinaman that turned a long way he was not a Test bowler, especially against batsmen prepared to use their feet.

Trueman had upset the locals in the MCC's warm-up match against the Combined Parishes when he struck Headley on the elbow. A public subscription raised in England, where Headley was living, had paid for his fare back to the West Indies in case he was required for the Test series. He had many admirers who thought 'The Master' was still up to playing for the West Indies. And, of course, he was still a national hero in Jamaica. He had been a great player and was known to some West Indians as 'the Black Bradman'. It was not a label that pleased him. I cannot say I blamed him. I do not think the Don would have taken to being called 'the White Headley'.

While the rest of the MCC players went to Headley after he had been struck to see how he was, Trueman walked purposefully back to his mark. In the West Indies we believed, and still believe now, that common cricketing courtesy dictates that the bowler should be one of the first to approach an injured batsman. Headley's status in the game, and his venerable age, should have made that course of action yet more certain. The crowd was enraged. They did not like to see 'Massa George' treated in such a shabby fashion.

This incident was quickly followed by another that was to convince us that Trueman may have had an over-inflated view of himself. Frank Worrell told me he had met Trueman in the hotel lobby and told him the finger he broke on the Commonwealth XI tour of India was troubling him, and he was unlikely to play. 'Oh well,' said Freddie, 'I have a sore heel and I am doubtful myself. So that makes it fifty–fifty.' How cheeky of him to compare himself with Frank!

Headley in for Worrell was a popular change, and when he came in to bat just before lunch on the second day of the opening Test I was at the other end. He was given a tremendous reception by a packed crowd. His Test debut had been twenty-four years earlier. It was a remarkable comeback. But what followed probably caused more bad feeling than any other incident on the whole tour. Hutton gave Headley a single off the last ball of the over, which meant he would have to face the last over before lunch. Hutton immediately called up Trueman, his fastest bowler. Had it been a normal over the crowd would not have minded so much, but it contained several bouncers and was very hostile. It was Test cricket at its most unrelenting. The feeling of bitterness was accentuated later when it was reported that Hutton said he had given Headley a single for old times' sake and because it was his last Test! It was a patronizing and unnecessary statement that only inflamed feelings.

After lunch, Hutton gave me a succession of singles early in overs to allow his bowlers to concentrate their efforts against Headley. George, however, was not disturbed by anything and we were all disappointed he was not able to make more than 16 before he was out to Lock. On that occasion it was not a blatant chuck!

Before the bottle-throwing Test in British Guiana Trueman was in more trouble. Turned down by the umpire in the British Guiana v. MCC match for an lbw appeal against Robert Christiani, the Yorkshireman made a remark that upset the official so much that he walked towards Hutton, fielding at leg slip, and made his feelings known. Hutton listened to what the umpire had to say and moved himself to mid-off to be closer to his bowler. At no stage did he try to speak to Trueman to give him a reprimand or advice about how to behave, and everyone was left with the impression that Hutton was not prepared to take the matter any further, which was regrettable.

Hutton's masterly 169 in the Bourda Test proved decisive, England winning by nine wickets. The matting pitch in Port of Spain on which the fourth Test was played had the reputation of being a batsman's pitch, and so it proved, with five batsmen scoring centuries in a high-scoring draw. The three Ws recorded three of them: Weekes 206, Worrell 167 and myself 124 in the West Indies' first-innings total of 681 for eight. Compton, with 133, and May, with 135, showed that England, too, had their champions.

Trueman went into that match having once again upset the local fans. This time he had bowled a bouncer at Trinidad's Wilfrid Ferguson, never known as anything other than 'Fergie', in the Trinidad v. MCC match. Fergie, living up to his image, went through the motions of playing a stylish hook. Highly displeased, Trueman responded with another bouncer that struck Fergie in the head and knocked him to the ground. In those days, of course, no one wore a helmet, not even number nine batsmen like Fergie. The crowd booed, and their mood was not improved when once again Trueman ignored cricketing tradition and strode back to his mark, leaving his colleagues to minister to the unfortunate Fergie.

Brian Statham bowled only nine overs in the Trinidad Test before retiring through injury, which was a big setback for the England team. I liked Statham. He was a fine bowler and a sportsman with it. Godfrey Evans missed out through illness and his place went to Warwickshire's Dick Spooner. There was another incident, when Tom Graveney, upset at his 'catch' off John Holt being disallowed, hurled the ball to the ground in anger. That would have qualified for a fine under today's code of conduct.

Nothing pleased me as much in that Test as my bowling figures of three for 52 in thirty-four overs. I bowled off-cutters, and in those favourable conditions for batting to go for less than 2 runs an over was some achievement. These were my best bowling figures in Test cricket up to that point, though there was little in the record books with which to compare them.

During the England first innings Frank King, our one bowler of pace, began bouncing Jim Laker and struck him a nasty blow over the eye that meant Jim had to be assisted back to the pavilion for treatment. In those days neither side had a physio and if there was no doctor around a stricken player would have to go to hospital. Jim was not a front-line batsman and, like Fergie, was the kind of batsman one didn't usually bounce because he was not a good enough player to defend himself adequately at all times. I did not think King's action was right because it left us open to the charge of descending to the same level as our opponents. Stollmeyer spoke to King and there was no repetition, but the damage had been done.

The West Indies needed only a draw to win the rubber in the fifth and final Test in Jamaica, but on a pitch that had more life in it than usual we mustered only 139 in our first innings. England went on to win by nine wickets to tie the series 2–2. Trevor Bailey was the destroyer of our batting, which appeared so strong on the scorecard that Garfield Sobers, making his debut at the age of seventeen as an orthodox slow left-arm bowler, was down at nine. As so often happens when a side thinks it has a powerful batting line-up, we failed dismally.

My 116 in our second-innings total of 346 was not enough for us to avoid defeat, but it was an enjoyable innings all the same, notable for a few amusing exchanges with Trueman. He bowled the usual quota of bouncers, some of which I hooked for four, and when he bowled a half-volley I drove it through to the cover boundary, but still ran. As I reached the exasperated and perspiring Trueman, he said, 'You won't get any f—ing more of those.' He was wrong.

Just before I reached my century a ball from Bailey bounced unexpectedly from a crack and struck me a painful blow on the wrist. Gloves then were pretty flimsy, filled with horse hair and offering little protection. While Trueman, as he still insists today, was as quick as any bowler before or since, Bailey could be sharp too. I had to depart after the close of play to have an X-ray. It revealed only bruising and I was able to continue. Laker, yet again, was the bowler who dismissed me.

Garfield Sobers took four wickets in this, his first Test match, and anyone who saw him would not have imagined they were looking at the cricketer who was to become the greatest all-rounder the game has known. The truth was that his slow left-arm, orthodox bowling was not out of the ordinary. But his pace bowling and his unorthodox Chinamen were definitely Test class. The fact that he realized all of his enormous potential delighted me and many other Bajans. He is acknowledged throughout the cricketing world as the greatest all-rounder and has proved himself to be one of our finest ambassadors. Another four years elapsed before he made his first Test hundred. It was the Test record score of 365 against Pakistan, and I was batting at the other end.

I got to know most of Hutton's side pretty well during that tour and have met most of them a number of times over the years. Trueman, in particular, is now a firm buddy, as he wrote in a copy of one of his books that he sent me. I played against him subsequently and found that he had matured a great deal. In 1954 he was still in the RAF and, as he said, 'hadn't been further than Cleethorpes' in his life. With better handling most of his problems would not have occurred.

Trevor Bailey, our chief tormenter in the final Test, was an amateur on that tour but was as competitive and tough a competitor as any hardened professional. He did not have a tremendous amount of natural ability, as he would admit himself, but he worked hard at his game and made the best use of his assets. He was not a sledger, though he attracted a few comments himself about his batting. His stalwart, defensive style, left foot firmly forward, brought many a remark along the lines of 'When is he going to play a shot?' We were always careful to speak out of earshot!

Len Hutton played one of his most memorable innings in the final Test, 205 out of a total of 414. He had been on the field for nearly three days in gruelling heat when he came in at tea having just passed the double century mark. He was greeted by a man standing near the gate. Not recognizing the well-wisher, he mumbled a word of thanks and carried on into the dressing room. He was not to know that it was the Prime Minister Alexander Bustamente and a moment or two later an official came into the dressing room accusing him of insulting the Prime Minister. The incident affected Hutton's concentration and he was out shortly after tea. Later that evening the two men met and Hutton apologized.

The *Daily Gleaner* devoted considerable space to the incident and Hutton wrote a letter which was published on an inside page. 'Had I been forewarned of the Chief Minister's presence, I should naturally have been delighted and honoured,' he wrote. 'I think it most regrettable that an unfortunate impression has been created and I hope this letter will make everyone realise that my team and myself have the greatest respect and admiration for the Hon. Mr Bustamente.'

But some people still saw it as a slight by the England captain, although my sympathies lay with Hutton. He gave his side of the affair in his book *Just my Story*, and no doubt that satisfied his critics. There was a remarkable passage in his book that read, 'the gradual exclusion of white folk is a bad thing for the future of West Indies cricket'. When the 1950 West Indian side went to England eight of the sixteen players were white. By the time of the 1953–4 series that total had been whittled down to a handful. The team was picked on merit and the change was inevitable. For the England captain to claim whites were being excluded implied discrimination against whites was taking place, and that was just not so. My feelings at the time were, 'Does he think that coloured people, on grounds of education or intelligence, are incapable of maintaining the traditions and standards of the game?'

It is significant that the West Indies teams, with a preponderance of coloured players, have a reputation for being cheerful and sporting tourists in victory or defeat. The West Indians have always tried to maintain the highest possible standards on the field, and that is reflected now in the figures of those punished under the ICC code of conduct. Not too many West Indians are ever up before match referees.

The MCC team Hutton brought to the Caribbean was all white, but most impartial judges would have had little difficulty in deciding which side did more harm to the game, theirs or ours. I was surprised to learn that, at a pre-tour briefing, Hutton's players had been told not to mix with the opposition. Freddie Trueman was the only player to lose his good-conduct bonus . . . which was even more surprising.

I have always been a strong opponent of a colour bar. The most important thing is that those running cricket should be the best people available, whatever the colour of their skin. In recent years there has been a swing towards commercial people being elected to the key positions on Boards in the Caribbean at the expense of those with a cricketing background. I do not think that is a good thing as there is a need for a combination of both. It is happening, too, in England and other Test-playing countries, with the trend being towards making money rather than making cricketers. The amateur officials who have kept cricket going in the face of stiff competition from other sports, people like my brother Keith, deserve every praise.

8 Guyana

One of the most satisfying periods of my life was between 1954 and 1970 when I went to live and work in Guyana, or British Guiana as it was known until it became independent in 1966. A few months after I took off from Barbados to emigrate there in 1954 the British government decided to suspend the constitution of British Guiana 'to prevent Communist subversion of the government and a dangerous crisis in both public order and in economic affairs'. Troops were landed to prevent public disorder. Friends warned me that the situation could be volatile but we stayed just the same.

The population at the time was less than half a million, in an area of 83,000 square miles, most of which was forest; it was very underpopulated. Nearly all the population lived in or around Georgetown, the capital, and most of the houses were built on stilts. This was because vast tracts of land were below sea level and in the rainy season there would be widespread flooding. The main export was sugar, and I was employed by the British companies responsible for planting, growing, cutting and producing sugar for sale abroad. Employees who had been indentured to the sugar companies were given loans to rent or buy wooden houses. My job was to develop cricket in the sugar plantations and improve the quality of Guyanese cricket in international competition. It was by far the most challenging task I had undertaken.

Facilities were poor. Most of the grounds had dirt pitches. Many of the employees were Indians, along with Africans, whose ancestors had been brought to the country by the British as slaves, and they now comprise 80 per cent of the population. The rest of the population are British, Dutch, Portuguese and Chinese, and it is one of the most cosmopolitan countries in the world. Only a few survivors of the aboriginal race, the Amerindians, remain. There is a large variety of religions, from every conceivable denomination of Christians to Muslims and Hindus.

Guyana is the only country in South America where the people speak English as their national language and play cricket on a regular basis to a high standard. Some cricket is played in Argentina, which is an associate member of the ICC. In Guyana, which is bigger in area than the British Isles, though smaller in population than Birmingham, the locals are fanatical about cricket, but in the mid-1950s, when I arrived and saw the facilities I realized what a mammoth task I faced to develop the game in the plantations.

I had to organize the clubs and the competitions and advise on improving facilities, persuading the owners to put down concrete pitches in the outlying areas that would survive the harsh climate. New grounds were built and such was the enthusiasm of the Indian population that immense strides were made in a very short time. There were several clubs on each estate and I decided to have them amalgamated into one club. If there were any disputes, I had to resolve them, and I remember one funny incident when a club protested that a game had finished too early. I invited the umpire who made the decision in to see me and asked him what time he called a halt. 'Five-thirty, sir,' he said. 'Did you have a watch?' I asked him. 'No, sir, but the train usually passes at five-thirty,' he said. I was not sure how he knew it was on time!

Some very talented players emerged at that time, including

Rohan Kanhai, Basil Butcher, Joe Solomon, Roy Fredericks and Lance Gibbs. All of them became established Test players and British Guiana soon became one of the better sides in the Caribbean. My first experience of managing the Guyana team was on a tour of Trinidad. On the outward-bound flight I collected the players' passports to fill in their immigration cards. Rohan gave me his passport and it said that his name was 'Babula'. Roy Fredericks's name was 'Roy Paul'. I said jokingly, 'We did not pick those players.'

The highlight for me was when I captained Guyana to victory in my native Barbados in 1963, winning by 24 runs. My contribution was 13 and 4, which was of little concern to me because we had achieved the victory. In the first innings I was a victim of Richard 'Prof' Edwards, the fast bowler from Wanderers who played five Tests against Australia and New Zealand in 1968. And in the second Charlie Griffith had me caught by Seymour Nurse. Both bowlers were quick. I learned later that Griffith, who began his career in the BCL (Barbados Cricket League) as a wicketkeeper–batsman, had considered me his hero in his earlier years.

Our success enabled us to confirm a brief period of supremacy in West Indian cricket. The win in Barbados was mainly due to Lance Gibbs, who took ten wickets for 86 runs in fifty-two overs. Barbados needed 122 to win and were spun out for 98, their lowest total at Kensington Oval for thirty-one years. I captained Guyana in thirteen matches, winning six and drawing five. At the time very little first-class cricket was played. My last games before retiring at the age of thirty-eight in 1964 were a victory against Jamaica and a drawn game against Trinidad and Tobago in Georgetown. In my twenty-two years of first-class cricket I played only 146 innings. Some idea of the disparity with English cricketers can be gauged from the fact that, in his twenty-three years of first-class cricket, Graham Gooch played 971 innings, while someone of my vintage, Tom Graveney, played 1223 innings, also in twenty-three years.

None of the cricketers on the estates were coached. They had natural talent, just as Shrivnarine Chanderpaul today has natural talent. My job was to guide them and advise them on how to make the best possible use of that talent. Until then only two cricketers from the interior had managed to break the monopoly of players from the Georgetown area in the British Guiana side, the opening bowler John Trim, who went on to represent the West Indies, and 'Sugar Boy' Baijnauth. Now they were to be followed by others.

There were a few mutterings when an outsider, me, became skipper, along the lines of 'They had to get in a Bajan to lead our team.' Some said that a Guyanese should lead the team out and then I could captain the side on the field. But the vast majority supported me and my work. I made many friends, and so did Muriel, who enjoyed our sixteen years in this exciting, friendly country. Eventually, the Guiana Sugar Producers Association appointed me as their social welfare adviser and one of my protégés, Joe Solomon, took over my cricketing role.

In 1958 the West Indies Board invited me to play in the Test series against Pakistan, informing me that they now considered me an amateur as I had a full-time job in British Guiana. An injured back kept me out of the second Test in Trinidad, but in the other Tests I hit 385 runs at an average of 96.25, including a century at Bourda, my new 'home' ground. It was my fifteenth and last Test century. That was the series where Gary Sobers made his world-record 365 not out at Sabina Park. We put on 188 together for the fourth wicket, a record against Pakistan that still stands. In what I thought would be my final appearance for the West Indies I made 47 and 62 in the last Test in Port of Spain which Pakistan won by an innings and 1 run. I was a victim in both innings of Nasim-ul-Ghani, the Pakistanis' ultra-accurate slow left-armer. Now he sits on the Cricket Committee of which I am chairman.

Fazal Mahmoud was a fine swing bowler but the rest of the Pakistan attack was average and it was a high-scoring series. In the first Test at Bridgetown Hanif Mohammed batted 858 minutes for his 337, the slowest triple hundred of all time. He was a very amenable person but not the sort of batsman you wanted to field to day in and day out. Like the best of the players from the East, he was quick-footed and judged the length of the ball brilliantly. Gary Sobers outscored him, playing a totally different type of innings, full of great shots.

In 1960, having considered my Test days behind me, I received an invitation to make a comeback after scoring a rapid 83 against the MCC in Georgetown. This time the Board said they would pay me as a professional again, which pleased me. West Indies needed someone to score quickly as we were one Test down and England would be on the defensive. My comeback was not the success I would have liked it to be. I mustered just 84 runs in three innings and both Tests I played in were drawn, leaving England 1–0 winners in the series. My last Test innings was 'caught Jim Parks, bowled Ken Barrington' for 22. Barrington was an occasional and sometimes erratic legbreak bowler who took just four wickets in that series.

England had some quality batsmen in the series, including Ted Dexter, a powerful player who hit the ball with tremendous strength, Peter May, Colin Cowdrey and Barrington. Freddie Trueman, by now much more mature, and Brian Statham were in their prime, and Ray Illingworth proved a doughty opponent. I had no regrets about retiring. I felt it was the right time and when a few months later Frank Worrell asked me to consider going on the tour to Australia, I declined.

One of my roles in Guyana was chairman of the National Sports Council; another was president of the Guyanan Cricket

Board. In one match, when I played under the captaincy of Steve Camacho, we won the Cup and I had to present the trophy. I ran to the dressing room to don my blazer and emerged to hand the trophy to Steve. It must be a precedent to have the president making the presentation to his own captain.

By 1970 there were racial and political problems in the country and Muriel and I decided it was time to return to Barbados. Three years earlier I had been presented with one of the country's national honours, the Golden Arrow of Achievement. One chapter in my life, as a cricket and social welfare adviser, was over and now I was to join the Barbados Shipping and Trading Company as a personnel officer, getting involved in trade union negotiations on behalf of the company. This negotiating role has helped considerably in my role as chairman of the ICC.

9   *At the Summit*

I reached the peak of my career in the 1955 series against Ian Johnson's Australian side, setting a number of records, some of which survive today. That series has gone down in the record books as being played in the 1954–5 season, but as the first Test started on 26 March 1955 that was not accurate. For some reason series in the West Indies are always given as spanning two years but nearly all of them take place in the early part of a single year.

I scored five centuries in the series, two hundreds in a single Test twice, and the most runs against Australia in a series abroad, 827, which was also the most runs scored in a Test series in the West Indies. It was the climax to a period when I recorded ten centuries in twelve Tests. At one stage I joined a group of six players with an average of over 60 in Tests. The others were Don Bradman, 99.94, Everton Weekes, 62.33, Neil Harvey, 61.73, George Headley, 60.83, and Herbert Sutcliffe, 60.73. I also became the second West Indian to pass 3000 Test runs. Everton Weekes was the first. I must have been a statistician's delight!

My image was of a huge, powerful man who wielded a large bat – similar to Clive Lloyd a generation on. But I can disclose now that the bat I used weighed just two pounds five ounces. That would be considered ridiculously light these days. Everyone then used a light bat. It was the balance that was important. The three-pounders used by Clive Lloyd, Graham Gooch and others were a long way off.

My bat was made by Lamberts, a small company in Nelson that I had been introduced to while playing Lancashire League cricket for Enfield. Players today are given contracts by bat makers to use their products and I have heard a figure of fifty thousand pounds mentioned. I did not receive a penny but I did get paid a royalty on every bat sold. As it was one of the smaller companies with a small market, I did not make a lot of money from the deal, but I did get complimentary bats. I had two rubber grips fitted to the handle and used a couple of bats each season. I tended to be a little superstitious. If I started well with one bat I tended to keep using it. In 1955 I must have used the same bat all season! All the bats were made in England in those days, with Gunn and Moore, Gray Nicholls and Stuart Surridge being the big companies.

I visited some of the factories, including Surridge's, in 1950 when we toured England. Stuart Surridge was just about to take over as captain of Surrey. Our game at the Oval against the county was our first in London and, keen to impress, we scored 537 for five, some players using the bats Stuart had given them at his factory a day or two before. Everton Weekes scored 232 and I made 128. The unfortunate Stuart's twenty-one overs cost 106 runs without a wicket. 'It's all your fault,' I joked. 'You shouldn't have given us those bats.' He was an exceptionally generous man.

In 1955 I still had a few problems with my back and was no longer keeping wicket. Most wicketkeepers are on the small side and had a shorter distance to travel when diving. I tended to hit the ground harder and it had a damaging effect on my back.

The difference in the two sides was the bowling, and it accounted for the Australians winning the series 3–0. Only one of our bowlers succeeded in taking more than ten wickets: Denis Atkinson, whose thirteen wickets cost 35.30. He was top of our bowling averages. Two bowlers, Frank Worrell and Frank King, our fastest bowler, had averages of 103.66 and 134.33, respectively, and took just three wickets apiece. Sonny Ramadhin took five wickets at 75.80 and Alf Valentine five at 69.80.

The Australian batting was dominant throughout with Neil Harvey, one of the best left-handers ever produced by Australia, averaging 108.33, and Keith Miller, going in at four, 73.16. Miller also took twenty wickets, the same as his partner Ray Lindwall, at the same average, 32. Lindwall and Miller were slightly past their best at the time but were still very fine bowlers. And they used plenty of bouncers to try to unsettle us.

Bill Johnston, so effective in England, hardly played, and nor did the injured Alan Davidson. Richie Benaud was top of the Australian bowling averages, with eighteen wickets at 27. He was a class leg-spinner who had plenty of variation.

Jeff Stollmeyer was the West Indies captain and, being uncertain of my fitness at the start of the series, he worked me hard in practice. He was so successful that I finished up my side's best bowler in the Australian first innings of 515 for nine in the first Test at Kingston. My three for 50 in twenty-six overs included three prize victims, Neil Harvey for 133, Keith Miller, with 147, and Richie Benaud, whom I bowled for 46. I was pleased with that. Stollmeyer asked me to come on first change after Frank Worrell had bowled only seven overs.

When we batted some of my team-mates found Lindwall difficult to handle, and my 108 was the top score in our 259. Collie Smith, in his first Test innings, helped me add 138 for the sixth wicket with his 44. He did even better second time out with a top-class 104. We still lost the match by nine wickets.

The Australians were popular wherever they went, the opposite to Len Hutton's English side of the previous year. They mixed well, and characters like Keith Miller enjoyed the repartee with West Indian crowds. These days most countries allow their players to have single rooms. On that tour Frank Worrell, Everton Weekes and myself often shared the same room. We were friends, not rivals. When we were staying at the Queen's Park Hotel in Port of Spain for the second Test we came back from a meal at 10.30 and heard some of the Australians playing cards in a nearby room. 'Come and join us,' said 'Nugget' Miller. We went in and were entertained lavishly. Soon Everton and I were joining in the card school. Frank never played cards but he was happy with the drinks. The 'party' lasted some time and I remember Everton promising them a bit of leather chasing the next day.

I scored 126 and Everton made 139 out of the West Indies' 382. Rain prevented a result but not before the top three in the Australian order, Colin McDonald, 110, Arthur Morris, 111, and Neil Harvey, 133, all scored centuries. I followed up with 110 in the second innings to become the third West Indian to score two centuries in the same Test. It was the first Test played on turf at Port of Spain and the pitch was an excellent one for batting. So great was the interest that on the opening day more than 28,000 people were crowded into the ground, a record at the time. They are just as enthusiastic now.

The third Test in Georgetown was equally one-sided, the Australians winning by eight wickets with a day remaining. Benaud was the main cause of our first-innings collapse, taking four wickets in twenty-three deliveries, and he followed up with a top score of 68 in his side's first innings. I reached 73 in our second innings before treading on my wicket taking off for a run off Lindwall. It was only the second time that had happened to me in my career.

The fourth Test in Bridgetown was remarkable for an astonishing performance by the Barbados wicketkeeper Clairmonte Depeiza on his home ground. He went into the game without having scored a first-class fifty. He joined Denis Atkinson when the West Indies were 146 for six, way behind the Australians' 668, and they added a world-record seventh-wicket total of 348 runs. Atkinson scored 219 and Depeiza 122. Depeiza's studious defensive forward push earned him the nickname 'the Leaning Tower Depeiza' from a local wit. A customs clerk, he had been hurriedly brought into the side after Jamaica's Alfie Binns and Cliff McWatt had been tried.

Lindwall and Miller and the rest of the Australian bowlers were so tired that Johnson did not enforce the follow-on and the match petered out into a draw, which was enough for the Australians to take the rubber.

The fifth and final Test in Kingston was a joyous one for me but not for the team. I scored two more centuries, 155 and 110, and rarely has the ball come off my bat more sweetly. Unfortunately, my records could not stop the Australians winning by an innings and 82 runs. Their innings of 758 for eight, the highest by a Commonwealth side, included no less than five individual centuries – McDonald, 127; Harvey, 204; Miller, 109; Ron Archer, 128; and Benaud, 121.

The Australians had an excellent wicketkeeper in the series: Gil Langley. He played a part in the dismissal of twenty batsmen and in the matches when he kept wicket conceded just 22 byes out of a total 2464 runs scored. And he equalled two records, with five dismissals in an innings and eight in a match. That was another area where we were outclassed.

We should have guessed that it was going to be an unrewarding series for the team when the skipper, Stollmeyer, injured a finger practising before the first Test and Atkinson took over even though the Three Ws were in the team. When he returned later, Stollmeyer injured a shoulder and dropped out again. His presence would not, I feel, have made too much difference.

10   *A Disastrous Tour*

I visited New Zealand at the end of the 1951–2 tour of Australia and enjoyed the experience. It is a good place to tour and the people are most hospitable. The pitches give the bowlers some help and for anyone aiming to play in England it is a useful training exercise.

When the West Indies' tour there of 1955–6 was looming I was asked whether I would be available and I stalled with my answer. These tours were primarily for younger players rather than established ones and I had been away from my job in British Guiana for a long time. My second son Ian, who is now an artist and also teaches art, had just been born. I was still thinking over the possibilities of going when the West Indies Board solved it for me by announcing a squad without my name.

A weakness of West Indian cricket at this time was our inability to find fast bowlers. This may seem strange, particularly as we were overladen with them twenty or so years later, and a bowler like Sylvester Clarke, as fast and menacing as any produced in the Caribbean, only played eleven times for the West Indies. Frank King was still around and was considered the number one despite his poor fitness record. The selectors called up a twenty-four-year-old sugar plantation worker from Jamaica, Roy Gilchrist, and he appeared to have some of the answers to the problem. He was pretty quick, about the same pace as Colin Croft, and with his long arms was capable of generating a lot of bounce.

Barbados was also about to launch a fast bowler, Wes Hall, and together with Gilchrist he made up the younger element in the party picked for the tour of England in 1957. So little cricket was played in the West Indies, particularly in those days, that the selectors held trials before picking squads for Test series. Although it could be a harsh way of selecting the team, there was little alternative.

I was playing in the second trial at Port of Spain when the names went up on the scoreboard. It was a rather painstaking way of announcing seventeen or so names and I was standing near Wes Hall, watching the expression on his face as it was done. He was speechless for one of the few times in his life until he finally saw his name go up then his face broke into a huge smile.

Gilchrist was a difficult cricketer for any captain to handle. He had the ability to be as quick as anyone and he was given every chance. He was uneducated and gave the impression that he felt everyone was against him. Another Jamaican, O'Neil Collie Smith, was included in the tour party and was the opposite in personality, an outgoing, popular young man who fitted in wherever he went. Collie came from one of Kingston's poorest districts and his Test debut against Australia in 1955 at the age of twenty-one came after playing just two matches for Jamaica. He was a player with flamboyant shots and was surely destined to break some of the records of the Three Ws. After the car crash in England in which he was killed 100,000 people turned out for his funeral in Kingston.

The SS *Golfito* set sail from Barbados in April 1957 with the Bajan members of John Goddard's squad and went south to pick up the Trinidadian and British Guianan contingents in Port of Spain before moving on to Jamaica to link up with the Jamaicans. In the three days we spent in Kingston we played a warm-up match. The journey from Bridgetown to England via the other islands took almost three weeks. Most of time was spent playing cards. Everton and I preferred bridge but there were plenty of poker and rummy schools as well. During the voyage, which was relatively smooth after a day or two of choppiness early on, I was called in by the joint managers, Tom Peirce and Cecil de Caires, and John Goddard, and was invited to become a member of the tour committee.

Everything appeared so serene and happy then, but shortly after our arrival in England it became apparent that there was not going to be a repeat of our success of seven years earlier. It turned out to be a disastrous tour, one of the most miserable ever undertaken by a West Indies side. Goddard was not worth his place and it soon became obvious that the balance of the side was affected by having to play him.

I think the joint managers felt I was angling for the captaincy because I had been successful when leading British Guiana to a number of victories. That was not the case. I thought Frank Worrell was the obvious choice, and so did the rest of the players. The experiment of having joint managers was not a success. Joint anything never works because responsibility for making decisions must rest with the one person, the manager.

De Caires was to upset me early in the tour when he claimed that, according to the press, I hadn't made enough effort to get fit after injury. Ramadhin and Valentine were still there with Sobers and Collie Smith's offbreaks to support them. The pace trio of Gilchrist, Tom Dewdney and Wes Hall was very inexperienced and Hall failed to make the first Test line-up because he was so erratic.

I went into the first Test match of the tour in pretty good form. In the MCC match we had to play on a green pitch against the bowling of Frank Tyson, then the fastest bowler around, and Alan Moss, who knew how to exploit conditions at Lord's better than anyone because it was his home ground. I felt at the time and now know that it was the best innings I ever played. I scored 117 in four and a half hours, starting out on a green top and having to adjust following rain to cope with different conditions. If I had to nominate one shot in my whole career which I thought was superior to any other, I would nominate a pull to midwicket for four off Tyson in that epic innings. The critics often award too much praise for big innings played on perfect batting pitches. True class comes out when conditions are awkward, and if you ask most great players to say which was their top innings they would probably follow my example and pick out one that was not necessarily a big score.

The outcome of the whole tour was decided on the final two days of the first Test at Edgbaston. England's use of what I still feel now was a dubious tactic that went against the true spirit of cricket earned them a draw after we were well on the way to an overwhelming victory. I do not use that as an excuse for our 3–0 defeat in the series. Our bowlers failed to perform at the level expected of them and the batting, with no one averaging more than Collie Smith's 39, wasn't good enough either. England's captain Peter May and his partner Colin Cowdrey stopped us winning with their record stand of 411 for the fourth wicket, but I have no hesitation in saying now that both these great batsmen were out lbw a dozen times or more but remained at the crease. This was because in those days umpires, particularly in England, did not give batsmen out on the front foot as there could be some doubt as to whether the ball would have hit the stumps. We lost count of the number of times May and Cowdrey put their left foot down the pitch, bat tucked inside the pad, to let deliveries from Ram and Val bounce away harmlessly off the pad. Later the MCC altered the lbw Law to allow bowlers to win the verdict if the ball pitches outside the line of the off stump when no shot is played, as long as the ball would have hit the stumps. I have always believed the batsman has a bat in his hands to hit the ball, not hide it behind his pad. I do not blame May and Cowdrey for what they did, though. It was permissible under the Laws as they stood at the time and gained them a draw from one of the greatest rearguard actions in cricket. But it was bad for the game and set a poor example to youngsters.

There had been few shots of any note in England's first innings when Ramadhin once more ran through their batting, seven for 49 in thirty-one overs being his best performance in Tests. It was a dreadful display of batting by a side containing such players as Brian Close, who opened, May, Cowdrey and Trevor Bailey. We succeeded in totalling 474 against an attack consisting of Statham, Trueman, Bailey, Lock and Laker. Has there ever been a better England attack, or a better-balanced one? I doubt it. We were overjoyed at seeing Collie Smith score 161. He was a very free-hitting player who picked the bad ball extraordinarily early. It was a great loss not just to West Indian cricket, but to the whole cricketing world when he died.

I scored 90 and pulled a hamstring muscle in the process which kept me out for three weeks. I scored the last 40 runs with Bruce Pairaudeau acting as my runner. He also acted as a runner later for Frank Worrell, whose injury prevented him from bowling in the second innings, another blow for us. It was the first time I had batted with a runner and it led to a lot of confusion. Several times I called for a run and set off before I realized I had to stay in my crease. Poor Bruce spent more time in the middle as a runner for me and Frank, who made 81, than he did for his own innings, which lasted only a few balls for 1 run.

England's second innings was in poor shape at 113 for three when Cowdrey joined May at the start of their memorable stand. Eight hours and twenty minutes later, with their pads no doubt punch-drunk from having taken so many blows, Cowdrey was caught in the deep for 154 and the stand was over. May went on to reach 285 not out before declaring at 583 for five. In hindsight, he probably regretted not declaring earlier, because the West

Indies finished a bewildering Test on 72 for seven and were perilously close to defeat. Frank Worrell and myself were both forced to bat lower down, again with a runner, and managed just 1 run between us. I took a quick shower and returned to my position in front of the away dressing room to watch those anxious final moments. Today's players usually watch the TV set in the dressing room. There was rarely a television at grounds in 1957.

We left Birmingham that night by train for Bristol, where we started a county match the next day. We were practically forced to put out a reserve side, we had so many unfit players.

In those days the treatment for a muscle injury was to fix an electric pad to the area to warm it up. These days it is the opposite: ice to take the blood from the area in the early stages. I had one or two injections before the second Test and it still wasn't right. I should not have played at Lord's. That was why I was upset when I saw Cecil de Caires quoted in a newspaper after the tour was over saying that Everton Weekes, who had sinus problems, and I had 'made no attempt to get fit'. He said this was the main reason why we lost the series and it came as a shock to both of us. The injury was still troubling me a month later, in the third Test.

When we arrived at Lord's for the second Test the talk was about the ridge at the Nursery End. There were some officials who tried to play it down. They did not have to bat at that end! If you bent down to ground level you could see the ridge on a fast bowler's length and I was told it was caused by a drain that ran across that part of the square. The result was that every player in this match, West Indian or English, who remained at the crease long enough to collect a few runs also collected a few bruises. Brian Close was fortunate that the West Indies performed so badly and he only had to go to the crease once, otherwise he might well have had more bruises on his body than he acquired many years later when Andy Roberts and Michael Holding peppered him and he posed stripped to the waist for an unforgettable picture.

Tests later revealed that there was a ridge. The offending part of the square was relaid and new drains were put in. We made the mistake of selecting Alf Valentine for this match on the strength of his ten wickets in the previous game against a Sussex side that included the well-known writer and critic Robin Marlar. In the Lord's conditions his place should have gone to another pace bowler. Valentine was little more than a passenger, bowling only three overs. It was some comedown for someone who had bowled more than one hundred overs in a Test against the same opponents seven years earlier.

Trevor Bailey bowled as well on that opening day as I had ever seen him and his seven for 44 led to us being dismissed by four o'clock on the first day for a dismal 127. Few bowlers could have used the conditions better.

We were short of openers and Rohan Kanhai, whose best position was number three, was required to face Statham and Trueman. His 34 was our top score. Not long before, I had been playing with Rohan for British Guiana. After he had passed his hundred I promised him a bat if he reached two hundred, which I said was the milestone all great players should achieve at some stage in their careers. Rohan failed by a few runs and was distraught when he returned to the dressing room in an exhausted state. I congratulated him and told him not to worry about failing to meet the target. He was a likeable and talented player and I was proud to have played a small part in his development.

The experienced Gerry Alexander was the first-choice keeper on that tour, but had to stand down to let Kanhai take over because we had to accommodate John Goddard in the side as captain. Kanhai was an ordinary keeper and it was another sign of how weak management had disturbed the balance of the side.

I had scored 14 when Bailey, bowling from the Pavilion End, dropped one a little short and I tried to pull it to leg. The ball hit the ridge, kept low, and I was trapped in front. Umpire Charlie Elliott had no problems with that one. The series used officials of the calibre of Sid Buller, Dai Davies and Elliott who were all top class. Then, as now, England has the best umpires in the world, mainly because it is the only country in the world with full-time professional umpires. That is why England has four officials on the ICC panel to the two of the other Test-playing countries. How long this situation will last I don't know. Of the present ones, I rate England's David Shepherd the number one, followed by Steve Bucknor from the West Indies.

Roy Gilchrist bowled splendidly in the last two and a half hours of play and England were only 7 ahead when play ended. They had lost four wickets including Tom Graveney and Peter May, both victims of Gilchrist. Graveney was a prolific scorer against the West Indies and that was one of the few occasions when he failed against us. For all his obvious talent, he had failed against other opponents and his place was in danger. He had been called into the squad for the first Test but did not play and was under pressure to succeed in what was seen as a final chance.

As England only batted once it would have been unfair had the selectors dropped him, and their good judgement in keeping him for the third Test on a batsman's pitch at Trent Bridge was justified because he compiled 258: his highest Test score. Patience is a much needed quality for selectors and it is becoming harder for them to show it with the increasing clamour from the media and public for change and new faces.

It seems to be in the nature of West Indian teams that sometimes we have a thoroughly bad day, and the second day of the Lord's Test was a prime example. No less than seven catches were dropped, and the ebullient Godfrey Evans was allowed to carve 82 in only 110 minutes. Peter Richardson, a left-hander with a sound temperament and the ability to deflect the ball out of the reach of fielders, scored 76, and Colin Cowdrey hit 152. Colin batted a very long time. Stylish and elegant he may have been, but he used his pads too much for my liking.

Our humiliation was complete when Freddie Trueman, no mean swiper of the ball, dispatched Valentine for three sixes over long-on in the one over. England led by 297 and our woes continued when opener Nyron Asgarali pulled a muscle and Collie Smith, promoted to open for the first time in his life, was out to a low delivery from Statham. Kanhai was caught for a duck off a flier and we knew that if the England bowlers kept finding the right spots the match would not go into the fourth day, disappointing thousands of fans who had bought tickets and would not have their money returned. It was another thirty years before cricket's long-suffering supporters in England finally won the concession of money back if there was no play.

At least we did not go down without a fight. Everton Weekes was magnificent. He was forced to retire to have treatment on a broken finger and when he returned to the crease was struck a painful blow on the right thumb. Bravely, he carried on, and his 90 was a courageous exhibition of skilful and aggressive batting. Gary Sobers, too, showed he had the temperament to go with his brilliant array of strokes, and his 66 delighted another packed crowd. When it was all over we sat dejectedly in the dressing room in virtual silence.

English cricket reached a peak around that time and it was rightly acclaimed as the best in the world. May's side had a mixture of hardened professionals who had the advantage of being able to play the game on a daily basis and players like himself, brought up on excellent batting pitches at the universities.

Today they say county cricketers play too much and need more rest and time to practise. The daily grind did not appear to harm such players as Trueman, Statham, Bailey, Lock, Laker and

Evans too much, nor the batsmen. I see from the 1958 *Wisden* that my friend M. J. K. Smith played sixty-three innings that season and scored 2125 runs. He was one of a group of eight players who scored more than 2000 runs in the season. Forty years later very few players get anywhere near 2000 runs.

The Hampshire and England seam bowler Derek Shackleton bowled 1217 overs that season, which is about three times as many as today's opening bowlers. Shackleton, a Yorkshireman with a dry sense of humour, was a typical English medium-pace bowler who took ten for 136 against us at Southampton in fifty-five overs. We were lucky he was not playing at Lord's.

While the complaint in England is that they play too much cricket, in the West Indies we play far too little. Most of those not signed to clubs abroad play at weekends for their clubs and in only a handful of games in the regional competition. When they are on tour some players might lack the stamina to play on a daily basis. (The Trinidadian spinner Dninath Ramnarine was an example of that in the 1998 tour of South Africa. Brian Lara asked him to bowl twenty-nine overs in succession and his shoulder cracked up under the strain.)

Why England fell from their number one spot to the lower half of the table in world cricket is not too difficult to explain. Once schools stop playing cricket the supply of talent dries up. The supply lines from the universities have also got in a tangle, with the major universities no longer allowing budding Cowdreys and Mays to devote their time to cricket. If boys are not going to play in backyards and open spaces like we used to, no one with natural talent is going to emerge. The English Cricket Board is trying to get youngsters interested by introducing Kwik cricket into primary schools, and though it is a laudable objective, I do not think it is the complete answer. It would be revealing to find out how many cricketers have played for the England Under-19 side who learned the game by playing Kwik cricket. To succeed in any sport, a youngster has to want to play it and devote time to it. The initiative has to come from him, not from a well-meaning coach.

We face similar problems in the Caribbean. There are so many other sports for boys, including the increasingly popular basketball, and they watch them on TV endlessly. Cricket needs heroes and there are not many: Lara is the only batting hero we have at the moment.

The third Test in 1957 offered us some respite. It was played in heatwave conditions which were to our liking and the pitch was as bland as any in the Caribbean. The unfortunate part was that Goddard lost the toss and we were condemned to almost two days in the field watching Graveney record his 258 and May scoring 104 in England's 619 for six. As one of the tour committee I knew how important it was to make a good start against such a strong bowling side and we changed the openers yet again. It was the turn of Gary Sobers to open. His partnership with Frank Worrell, another makeshift opener, put on 87 for the first wicket. Worrell went on to make a sublime 191, a masterpiece of an innings. He was the first West Indian to carry his bat through an innings in a Test, and ultimately was on the field right through to Monday afternoon, almost four days. Our 372 was inadequate, though, and when following-on we made only 367. Collie Smith's outstanding 168 was the high point, but England knocked off the runs they needed to win by nine wickets.

At Headingley Goddard won the toss in the fourth Test and decided to bat on a typically green pitch which proved just right for Peter Loader, the stand-in for Statham. Loader had a slightly odd action, and when he pushed for extra pace there were those who thought it might have been suspect. There was little sign of that on the opening day because the conditions were so favourable he did not have to strain for pace. The match went into the history books because he took a hat trick at the end of the innings to record his best figures of six for 36. An even greater achievement would have been to dismiss the Three Ws in the same over and he came close to doing it. He yorked Frank Worrell with his second ball in an over, bowled Everton Weekes two balls later and, facing his next, I glanced the ball towards May at short leg and he nearly caught it.

Worrell was our most effective bowler with seven for 70 in England's 279. A feature of that innings was that the three Varsity players, May, Cowdrey and the Revd David Sheppard, scored 69, 68 and 68, respectively. I liked Sheppard; he was a useful player but not in the same class as May and Cowdrey. He had the luck on his side in that innings, and several of our players asked him how they could become priests, because they wanted that kind of advantage. As a man and a cricketer, he set a fine example.

Our second innings totalled only 132 and we lost by an innings and 5 runs. Ramadhin was last man out. He played the ball to Sheppard close on the legside and set off for an impossible run as the Sussex fielder threw him out. As Ram walked into the pavilion, Valentine, who was not playing, said to him, 'I am surprised at you, Sonny. Trying to steal a run in front of the Reverend. Don't you know the commandment "Thou shalt not steal?"' David Sheppard told this story when preaching at a Sportsmen's Service in Leeds the next day. 'I am pleased to hear that at least one member of the West Indies team knows the Commandments,' he told his listeners.

And so on to the Oval for the final Test in this miserable, for us, series. We were horrified when we saw the pitch. It was powdery and very dry and our fears were realized when the first delivery of the match, from Frank Worrell, landed and a puff of dust came up. The groundsman said that a dressing of marl 'had not taken' but to us it appeared a pitch especially prepared for Lock and Laker. That was how it worked out. They took sixteen wickets between them and we lost by an innings and 237 runs.

Ram bowled manfully and we missed Valentine, who was not playing after having broken his nose. Goddard went down with flu after the first day and I took over as captain. It was the first time I had skippered the West Indies. I did not give the batsmen advice on how to play. I left it to them. The conditions were so weighted in favour of spin that to decide on passive defence or bold stroke play had to be a personal decision. We were bowled out for 89 in the first innings and 86 in the second.

Poor Everton was out for a pair, the first time it had happened to him. An unusual fact about his career was that he hit only one six. It was a straight drive off a no-ball bowled by the Australian Bill Johnston. 'I grew up playing cricket in the backyard and you had to keep the ball down to avoid upsetting the neighbours,' he told me. 'If it went over the palings they often used to keep it and the game had to come to an end. We didn't want that.'

I had to make the speech at the end of the series, and except for congratulating Peter May and his players there was little I could say. May said: 'I don't know if there is an answer to Lock and Laker on a wicket like this.' I know there isn't, but there must be a better way of preparing pitches. Three of the five in the series were suspect and each time we came off worse.

This time there was no grand welcome in Bridgetown Harbour when we returned. I was elected one of the five Cricketers of the Year for 1957 and I can only imagine it was for past achievements prior to the first Test in England.

11   *Skirmish at Sion Mills*

One of the lowest points in West Indian cricket came on 2 July 1969, when we played Ireland at Sion Mills, near Londonderry in Northern Ireland. The Troubles were just starting in the province and they started for us that day. I was manager of the West Indies team that had just escaped from defeat in the second Test at Lord's the day before and we had to pack our bags quickly and fly from Heathrow to Belfast that night. It was not a clever piece of scheduling but, having agreed to the tour conditions, we had to accept it. Some of the leading players, including Gary Sobers, Lance Gibbs and Clive Lloyd, did not go and I decided to play at the age of forty-three. Basil Butcher was captain.

When we arrived at Sion Mills it had been raining and the pitch was wet. Butcher conducted the toss near the pavilion and, when he called correctly, decided to bat. As he announced what was happening to the other players, Jackie Hendriks, the wicket-keeper, said, 'Skipper, have you looked at the wicket?' Hendriks thought we should have put Ireland in. But none of the players really wanted to field, having had such a tiring journey, so Joey Carew and Steve Camacho went out to face two bowlers named O'Riordan and Goodwin who were about to make history. Wickets tumbled like wheat stalks under a combine harvester. It was 4 for six, then 6 for eight and soon 12 for nine. At this total Camacho ran inside the dressing room shouting, 'We're now 13 for nine. We've got a bye!' I managed to last a few balls and my 6 was the highest score of the recognized batsmen.

As it was not a first-class match these scores were not included in our records, fortunately. The last pair of Grayson Shillingford and Philbert Blair hung around for a while and Grayson, who made 32 runs on the whole tour, hit a couple of fours. We were all out for 25. That was only a third of the previous lowest total ever recorded by the West Indies: 76 against Pakistan in 1959. (In 1986, Pakistan would dismiss the West Indies for just 53.)

Goodwin, the Irish captain, took five for 6 and O'Riordan four for 18. As the correspondent in one newspaper wrote, 'Both bowled medium pace on a reasonable length and the pitch did the rest.' Ireland won by nine wickets, and although the match was not deemed first class, *Wisden* still included the scorecard in the 1970 edition. While we were waiting at the airport for the flight back for our next match against Glamorgan in Swansea, there was the usual announcement about 'Would passengers with children please board the plane first' and I said, 'Let's go, lads, that's us!'

That 1969 visit to England was a half tour. We shared the summer with the New Zealanders. It was the first time the West Indies had undertaken such a tour. Results were acutely disappointing with a 2–0 defeat in the three-Test series and only three matches won out of the twenty-two played. I was a selector at the time and there were five selectors in all, representing the five territories who took part in the West Indian regional competition. The Leeward and Windward islands fielded a combined side.

I persuaded Jeff Stollmeyer, president of the Board, to ask his fellow members to reduce the selection committee to three and that duly happened. This was a more manageable committee and it also meant that the members would be less likely to press for the inclusion of their own players. Generally, when someone spoke in glowing terms of a player not from his territory I always took note. When they spoke of their own players I did not listen so intently.

I was hankering to return to Barbados after my spell in Guyana and I spoke to Sir Anthony Murray, who had numerous contacts in Barbados. Soon after I received a letter from the chief personnel officer of the Barbados Shipping and Trading Company asking me to attend an interview. I was offered a position as personnel officer and accepted. It was a good decision because I was promoted to chief personnel officer and later became a director of the company, the first black man to be appointed an executive director.

It was a large company with over three thousand employees. The company was always understanding when I asked for time off to manage West Indian sides abroad and would invariably give me permission to go. I always had to forfeit my four weeks' annual leave and, of course, being a manager in those days was an unpaid job.

For many years I was a senior vice-president of the Barbados Cricket Association. Peter Short was president and I was asked to stand against him on a number of occasions but always declined as he was doing a fine job. The West Indies Board appointed him as my assistant manager and treasurer in 1969 and we worked well together. He stood in for me on one occasion, the match late on against Hampshire at Southampton. Our fellow Bajan Roy Marshall was still playing for Hampshire but he missed that match with a fractured finger and acted as liaison officer instead. He was a good choice. That was only one of two county games that we won and we did it despite two magnificent innings by the South African opener Barry Richards, 86 in the first innings and 120 in the second. His enforced absence from Test cricket was a big loss to the game.

At lunch Peter and Roy were seated next to Field Marshal Viscount Montgomery and Peter described their conversation to me. Roy: 'Mr Short served in the British army, sir.' Monty: 'Oh, what rank?' Peter: 'I was a captain, sir.' Monty: 'Well, we weren't exactly the same rank then, were we?' Peter was very amusing about the great military commander. 'He also confided his thoughts about democracy,' Peter recalled. 'He said democracy will destroy itself. You need someone to give the orders. I think he had himself in mind.'

The West Indian side that year was a much changed and weakened one. Eleven of the sixteen were newcomers to the Test scene in England. Seymour Nurse, Rohan Kanhai, Conrad Hunte, Wes Hall and Charlie Griffith were all absent and only Gary Sobers, the captain, Lance Gibbs, Basil Butcher, Joey Carew and Jackie Hendriks remained of the successful 1966 squad. Never had the West Indies been more dependent on Gary. He had just played eighteen months of continuous cricket, including his first summer of county cricket in England with Nottinghamshire, following the lifting of the ban on overseas players and he was physically exhausted. In the three Tests he scored only 150 runs for an average of 30. He had problems with a knee and shoulder and his bowling showed a similar decline in effectiveness to his batting.

The attack of John Shepherd, who had back problems after being overworked at Lord's, Grayson Shillingford and Vanburn Holder was not one of our strongest. With Hall and Griffith no longer in the reckoning, we had to find others, and it proved a difficult task for a few years. Lance Gibbs was nearing the end of his career and took only six wickets in the series.

England's team was superior, including fellows such as John Snow, Derek Underwood, David Brown, Barry Knight, and Ray Illingworth, one of a number of tough Yorkshiremen in their side. As a captain, Illingworth was thoroughly professional and unrelenting. And he had another tough Yorkshireman to rely upon at the top of the order, Geoff Boycott. He was an exceptionally good player, and over the years I managed West Indian sides he was the opposing batsman I wanted to see dismissed more than any other. He would frustrate the bowlers and hold one end up. It may not have been exciting but it stopped us winning. He was never short of confidence. I remember arriving at a ground and saying to him, 'There's a good crowd in today.' 'There would be three times as many if I was playing,' he replied.

Gary had a trying time as captain. And he wasn't around that much with the rest of the players after close of play. He was too great a cricketer to be a captain because he always expected everyone to perform as he did, and that was not possible. One day an old lady came up to me and said she was trying to learn something about the game. She'd been told the fielders were there to stop the ball but could not understand why most of them seemed to be behind the wicket, in the slips and gully area when the ball was being hit in front of the batsman.

One problem with Gary's captaincy was that, when things were going badly, he would come on to bowl himself. He expected things to happen every time he was involved in the action.

The Guyanese Basil Butcher finished top of the batting averages in first-class games and Clive Lloyd not far behind him in the Test averages, with another Guyanese, Roy Fredericks, in third place. Fredericks was a brilliant hooker and I think I may have had a hand in his emergence as a Test player when I had him in one day for a chat. 'Why is it you get a good forty or so and then get out?' I asked him. 'Great players go on and pass a hundred, then two hundred.' He was a heavy smoker and I told him, 'I don't think you are fit. When you've been out there a couple of hours you are exhausted. You've got to get yourself much fitter.' I think he took my advice. My philosophy as a manager was to chastise in private and praise in public. I did not think it was a good managerial ploy to criticize a player with the others listening. My training at the Industrial Welfare Society, now known as the Industrial Society, proved invaluable.

I was lucky with the weather on most of my tours to England and this one was no exception. The sun shone from early June right through to the end of the tour. Maybe some rain would have helped us at Manchester in the first Test because after Illingworth won the toss we were well beaten by ten wickets. Dropped catches allowed Boycott and the rugged John Edrich to record a century opening stand before Edrich was sent back by his partner and run out for 58. Boycott went on to score 128 out of England's 413. In reply we managed only 147. John Snow, an impressive bowler with a high action, took four wickets, as did David Brown.

Our total clearly wasn't enough and Illingworth took the positive step of enforcing the follow-on. I rated him one of the leading England captains I encountered and he was not a cautious leader, in spite of what some of his critics suggested. Only Fredericks, with 64, passed fifty in both of our innings and England duly completed their first win at Old Trafford for eleven years.

There was no rest for the tourists in those days. We got into the coach and drove down the old A6 and A1 to Nottingham for a game against Gary Sobers's county side the next day.

The second Test at Lord's saw Jack Hampshire become the first Englishman to record a century at Lord's on his debut there. His feat was matched by Charlie Davis, the Trinidadian who was making his debut, for us at Lord's. Charlie was just the upright, sound number three batsman a side of strokeplayers needs in its ranks. He played straight and displayed a fine temperament. He was ruffled, however, when his mistake resulted in Sobers being run out for 29 at a vital moment in our first innings of 380. The ball ran off Sobers's pad just behind square leg and Charlie called. Gary set off only for Charlie to scream, 'No.' Boycott raced in from square leg, picked the ball up and kept his head by running on to the wicket and whipping off the bails with the ball still in his hand. Charlie dropped his bat and threw up his hands in horror.

At the next interval Sobers showed what a generous and magnanimous cricketer he was throughout his career. Charlie had a reputation for being a little fiery: when he was out he would come into the dressing room with his bat swinging around in his hand and he would even occasionally let go of it when particularly enraged. The players often felt it was advisable to leave or hide behind chairs or tables. Before he could react this time, Gary went up to him and said, 'Don't let that worry you. It was totally my fault.' You could see the sense of relief in Charlie's face. He went out after the break and continued batting with confidence, his innings lasting more than six hours. We made a point of all of us being on the balcony to applaud him when he reached his century.

A supreme effort by Sobers, bowling at close to his fastest, reduced England to 61 for five before the Yorkshiremen took over, with Hampshire reaching 107 and Illingworth his first Test hundred of 113. Sobers pulled a muscle in the field and Illingworth allowed him a runner when he came in to bat. Gary declared at 295 for seven, setting England 332 to win in five hours, plus twenty overs. In a three-match series it was necessary to take risks to win if you were trailing. England made no effort to get the runs. Boycott, who finished with 106, took two and a half hours to reach his fifty.

The England selectors had surprisingly left Derek Underwood out, but he was back for the final Test at Headingley, and after not bowling a single over in the first innings, which was dominated by England's seamers, he proved the match winner at the end, taking four wickets. He was a mean bowler and in English conditions was often the difference between defeat and victory. The number of bad balls he delivered was minimal. His accuracy was unmatched by anyone, anywhere.

A turning point in our second innings was when Sobers played a head-in-the-air shot against Barry Knight and was bowled for a duck. Butcher, on 91, was our last hope of winning but he went to a catch by Alan Knott off Underwood that *Wisden* reported was 'disputed'. I do not recall any dissent. We might not have agreed with the decision but I don't think we showed it. Knott took six catches in that match to confirm my impression that he was right up there with Godfrey Evans as England's number one wicketkeeper of all time. He was a fitness and food fanatic and never stopped trying to improve his technique. He is still involved now as the coach to the England wicketkeepers and you can see his influence.

The Headingley Test was a dour affair and was watched by an abnormally small total crowd of fifty thousand over the five days. Yorkshiremen are careful with their money and they know their cricket.

We played two more matches, at Leicester and Hampshire, and departed the scene to let the New Zealanders take over. The results had been poor. But it was still an enjoyable trip, and it was a useful learning exercise for the younger players.

12 *Selector*

In my twelve years as a West Indian selector picking the side was not too difficult because the West Indies had nine or ten outstanding cricketers. The problem was choosing the one or two players to complement them. I was dining with Jeff Stollmeyer in Trinidad once at a time when there was a controversy about whether Trinidadian Larry Gomes should play. Halfway through the meal a waiter brought a note to the table addressed to me. I read, 'No Larry Gomes. I hope the chef puts arsenic in your food.' It was signed by a local racehorse owner. I did not reply. These days it would merit a court action. It highlighted the problem of parochialism in West Indies cricket. Some think the players in their island or territory should be picked first.

That was a minor incident compared with what happened when we decided not to play Gary Sobers in the 1973 home series against the Australians. Gary had had several operations on his knee and it was a miracle that he managed to play eighty-seven Tests in succession and ninety-three in all. After his second operation in 1972 the surgeon told him he was surprised he was still able to play cricket. The bones were rubbing against each other and were flaking away. Gary certainly paid a very high price for his sporting fame. He was playing for Nottinghamshire at the time and cricket was almost a year-round job for him.

The West Indies Board usually pays the air fare of the players who are resident in England whom they want to return home for a Test series. Realizing he might not be fit, Gary called Cecil Marley, the president of the Board, and told him he was resigning as captain because he was not fit. Asked whom he recommended to take his place, he nominated his cousin David Holford, with Clive Lloyd and Rohan Kanhai his second and third choices. The Board decided that Rohan was the man, and I think we made the right choice.

Two weeks before the first Test I called Gary and asked how his knee was progressing and he said that he had been doing plenty of exercises and felt confident about being ready for the second Test. He played for Barbados against Trinidad and bowled twenty overs, claiming he was fit. Jeff Stollmeyer disagreed and told him the selectors wanted him to play against the tourists the following week to make sure of his fitness. 'I don't want to be on trial,' said Gary. 'Give a young player a chance.' Stollmeyer then suggested that Gary should see the Board's doctor to obtain clearance as this was Board policy. Gary admitted in his autobiography that he lost his temper at this point. 'No doctor could tell me about my fitness,' he said. 'I knew whether I was fit enough to play. I hadn't missed a single Test for eighteen years and they must have known I played sometimes when I wasn't fit and no doctor would have passed me to play.'

A few days later I met Gary at the match against the Australians. I told him the selectors wanted him to play and invited him to a two-day practice game with the rest of the squad in St Vincent. 'You know where you can put your practice game,' he said angrily.

Gary never played in the series and the West Indies lost it 2–0. Dennis Lillee broke down with a back injury and Max Walker, known as 'Tangles' because of his ungainly action, was the bowler who took most of the wickets. He was a medium–fast swing bowler who proved that this type of bowling can be very effective on Caribbean pitches.

There was uproar throughout the West Indies about Gary's omission. Prime Ministers became involved and sixty-four leading sportsmen petitioned the Prime Minister of Trinidad, Dr Eric Williams, to have the matter brought up at the Heads of Government Conference in Guyana. Dr Williams said in his speech, 'I happen to think that Mr Sobers is one of the authentic folk heroes produced by the West Indian people. Mr Sobers [seems to] have been dealt with . . . in the typical West Indian fashion we discard at the wayside an old car that has been smashed up in a road accident. I regret it. If I had been involved in any way, it would have been handled differently.'

The radio phone-ins hummed with the voices of angry callers and the newspapers were full of letter-writers airing their criticisms. I did not receive any hate mail but it was a fraught time for me and the other selectors. Ian Chappell sided with the general public when he said victory over a West Indies side without Sobers was 'hollow'.

We experienced another problem in that series that reflected the way political interference can affect West Indian cricket. This time the player concerned was Clive Lloyd, who was playing for South Melbourne in Australia at the time. Forbes Burnham, the Prime Minister of Guyana, whom I knew well, believed that Lloyd should be playing in the series and wrote to Gough Whitlam, the Prime Minister of Australia, asking him to use his influence to allow Lloyd to be released from his contract. Lloyd returned to his home in Manchester and was told by Sir John Carter, the Guyanese High Commissioner in London, that the Guyanese government was paying his air fare home. Even Lloyd was surprised by this development. In effect, he was being sponsored by his own government. He played a couple of matches for Guyana and was included in the squad for the first two Tests.

Lloyd was involved in the practice sessions before the Barbados Test and obviously thought he stood a good chance of taking over from Sobers as captain. But we wanted someone who could bowl as well as bat and went for Bernard Julien, the Trinidadian who bowled left-arm over the wicket at roughly the same pace as Gary. Unfortunately, Julien was struck on the arm in practice and was forced to withdraw. Our decision to bring in Keith Boyce infuriated Lloyd, who proceeded to smash a ball through a dressing-room window and break down and cry. He told me he would not be twelfth man and also refused to line up with the rest of the players to be presented to the governor-general. He felt he had been victimized because he was sponsored by his government. I sat him down and told him he had a great future, possibly as West Indies captain, and urged him not to throw everything away on a false belief. We were not concerned that his prime minister was pushing him. Boyce was chosen because we wanted a bowler who could bat, rather than a batsman who only bowled a little. Wes Hall made similar comments and Lloyd finally agreed to stay on. He was chosen for the third Test in Port of Spain where, because the pitch was expected to turn even more than usual, we selected no less than four spin bowlers. Clive opened the bowling!

He had trouble with his contact lenses at the time, dust constantly getting into his eyes, and his indifferent performance with the bat led to him being barracked by the Trinidadian crowd. He was back wearing his more familiar horn-rimmed glasses on his home ground at Bourda in Guyana, and with the crowd on his side scored 178 before a second-innings collapse saw the Australians winning by ten wickets to clinch the series.

When the final Test took place back at Queen's Park Oval, the Caribbean's largest ground, the fans stayed away and the match was played in a very low-key atmosphere. The series had been full of problems for selectors and administrators alike. As selectors, we had also been given a hard time in Trinidad for omitting the local player Charlie Davis.

Rohan Kanhai was a sound captain, a good tactician and know-ledgeable about the game. His field placing was studied and usually correct. But whereas Lloyd would prove to be popular with his players, Rohan somehow lacked that rapport and his mood could change suddenly.

The relations between the West Indian and Australian sides was as good as I have ever experienced in Test cricket. I persuaded the ground authorities to let the respective managers introduce their players before the start of play and the crowd enjoyed it. We tried to do it in a jocular manner, mentioning the nickname of each player as well. It proved such a successful innovation that I was surprised it was never used again. It helps the public to identify with the players and is something I believe we should reintroduce. Up to that series the camaraderie among players had been on the decline but we succeeded in reversing that sad state of affairs. When enjoying the company of the Australians we could forget our problems about selection, government inter-ference and everything else.

There was less of a problem in the next series, our tour to England in 1973, when Gary Sobers said he would not be available to take any part because he wanted to be fair to Nottingham-shire. It was a position the selectors and the Board were happy to accept. Gary went on to make his final Test appearance in the return series in the Caribbean the following winter, when this greatest of all cricketers was dismissed for a duck in his first innings by Tony Greig and bowled for 20 in the second by one of the few full tosses bowled by Derek Underwood in his whole career.

There have only been two occasions in my time when the Board has overruled the selectors over the appointment of a captain: the first was before the 1974–5 tour of India, when our recommendation that Rohan Kanhai, then approaching forty, should continue in the job was rejected and Lloyd appointed instead; the second was in 1998 when the selectors recommended Courtney Walsh and the Board again went for youth and picked Brian Lara. The decision to select Lloyd turned out to be correct. He was thirty and had recovered full fitness after cracking a bone in his back while fielding, an injury that could have ended his career. His captaincy was lacking in several departments at first but he matured very quickly. In that series in India all five Tests produced results, three victories for the West Indies and two for India, with Lloyd himself sealing the series triumph at the Wankhede Stadium in the last Test with an unbeaten 242. When he reached 200 a lone spectator, a young man, came on to the pitch to congratulate him and a riot ensued after the police beat him with their sticks. The players had to return to the dressing rooms and half an hour's play was lost. The crowd of fifty thousand was so impressed with Lloyd and his players that they demanded they come back out to receive more applause. That was a happy, if long, tour, with Lloyd full of praise for his manager Gerry Alexander. It was a good lead in to the World Cup later in the year.

For the selectors, there was satisfaction to be gained from the choice of three young men who were to become among the greatest of West Indian cricketers – Viv Richards, Andy Roberts and Gordon Greenidge. The choice of Greenidge, who was brought up in England, was criticized at the time, but we were proved right.

Of course, for those great players to emerge, others must step down and, traditionally, West Indian cricketers are not too graceful when they finally have to accept retirement. Many of them are very bitter about it. They also tend to be very upset when they are omitted from Test squads. They think that they will not be recalled and that is the end of their Test career. It is true that there are fewer changes in West Indian squads but that is because we have a smaller pool of players than, for instance, England. The situation is the reverse there. England has between 350 and 400 professionals and the selectors are always making changes, which can be disruptive to continuity and team spirit. The rule of selection in the West Indies is that once you identify those players with class, you stick with them. That was what I tried to do in my years as a selector.

13   *World Cups and a*
   Possible Hat Trick

The night before the final of the inaugural World Cup in 1975, sponsored by the insurance company Prudential, the West Indies team had a meeting at their hotel in Kensington and I asked them what time they felt they should go to bed. As manager, I hadn't imposed a curfew, because that hadn't been my practice during any of the many tours I managed. One player said, 'Manage [their nickname for me], are you putting a curfew on us?' 'No', I said. 'I just want your input. I want to know what you think is a reasonable time.' There was some discussion. Some felt 11.30 was a good time, others 10.30 and the majority seemed to favour eleven o'clock. One of the senior players, Lance Gibbs, suddenly said, 'I don't know why we are talking about this, the tour committee has already decided on eleven o'clock.' That was true but Lance's comment took me aback. I explained later that it was a tactic to reach a consensus on a management decision rather that just announce what had been decided. So eleven o'clock it was, and everyone was on time in the morning.

In my tours as West Indian manager there were a few instances of players staying out to unreasonable hours. On those occasions I called them in for a chat and a warning. I was known as a disciplinarian and there were never any re-offences from players after they had seen me! I am not suggesting that all of the players always returned to their hotel on time. For instance, Gary Sobers often was out late, but it never affected his playing.

In those days we spent less time practising and exercising than is the case with the modern players. After our exciting victory by 17 runs a lot was made of our fielding, the ground fielding in particular. Five Australians were run out, including both Chappells, and it was a key factor in our success. But we did not have a long session practising our fielding that day, or on any day in the two-week tournament. We just had some exceptionally talented fielders.

I was working as chief personnel officer at the Barbados Shipping and Trading company when I was invited to manage the West Indies squad in 1975. I had four weeks' leave and took it to accompany the team to England in an unpaid capacity. It was an honour to do so. In the West Indies our cricketers play a lot of one-day cricket, usually forty overs, and it was no hardship to play in a sixty-over tournament. When the Gillette Cup started in England in 1963 each side had sixty-five overs and not many matches failed to end in a day. The ICC has now agreed that fifty overs is the ideal number and that is used uniformly around the world.

With players like the captain Clive Lloyd, Viv Richards, Gordon Greenidge, Rohan Kanhai, Alvin Kallicharran and Andy Roberts, I felt we had a very good chance of winning the first World Cup. We picked our best players, not players we thought were one-day specialists. Australia started the practice of selecting one-day specialists and England copied it. I do not think it is needed. There might be the odd cricketer who excels in the short form of cricket and is not so successful in Test matches; Collis King comes to mind. But in the main I believe you have to stick with your best players and I think we were proved right to do so. We won that tournament and the one in 1979 and I think we might well have made it a hat trick in 1983 had I remained in charge for a third time. I was expecting to be manager in 1983 but the Board decided to give the job to their chief executive, Steve Camacho. As he was a protégé of mine and a long-time friend, I had no criticism of their decision, but I felt that the team would have benefited from the continuity of having Clive Lloyd and me once again. The West Indies unexpectedly lost to India in the 1983 final because we started out chasing a low total too quickly. I was frantic, wanting to go into the dressing room to tell them to hold back, but I decided against it.

Our first match in 1975 was against Sri Lanka. They were a long way from the outstanding quality of their present one-day team. We won by nine wickets with almost forty overs in hand after bowling the Sri Lankans out for 86 at Old Trafford. Keith Boyce, the Bajan all-rounder who had a successful county cricket career with Essex, took three for 22. He was a gifted one-day cricketer, fast and straight as a bowler, hard hitting with the bat and dynamic in the field, with a powerful long throw. When he retired he became a very hard drinker, and it was to his credit that he recovered and went on to do excellent work as a coach helping in the development of the game in Barbados.

There are other West Indian cricketers who have known fame but cannot cope with life when the good times end and have taken to drink. Sadly, Keith Boyce died in 1998 at the age of fifty-five. Bernard Julien, the Trinidadian all-rounder from Kent, played in the 1975 tournament and he, too, had a few problems. A left-arm bowler, he had a lot of potential which, to a certain extent, he did not fulfil.

The West Indies' second game in their group was the most exciting in the tournament. We won by one wicket, with the winning run coming off the fourth ball of the last over. It was a classic one-day game with our last pair Deryk Murray, 61 not out, and Andy Roberts, 24 not out, taking the score from 203 for nine past Pakistan's 266. I had almost given up and was downstairs waiting for the official presentation to take place. But I did have my fingers crossed! Murray was a capable batsman with a sound temperament who scored many valuable runs for his side in company with the tail-enders. Roberts showed the value of having tail-enders in your side who could play straight and not throw their wickets away.

The Pakistani opening bowler Sarfraz Nawaz was voted Man of the Match by Tom Graveney. Sarfraz was a very capable bowler who moved the ball and got a lot of lift. He was a talkative character on and off the field and I see he is still provoking arguments to this day.

Each side in the two groups had to play three matches, and our final opponents were Australia, then captained by Ian Chappell. The Australians had already won their opening two matches and, like us, were through to the semi-finals. But they wouldn't have been pleased about the way we beat them by seven wickets with four overs to spare. Alvin Kallicharran took 35 off ten deliveries from Dennis Lillee in his 78, and the great Australian bowler conceded 66 runs in ten overs. Boyce was another key figure for us, dismissing both the Chappell brothers in six balls. There were no restrictions on bouncers in the first World Cup and there was a liberal supply, chiefly from Boyce. It was not a good tournament for the Chappell brothers. They have been compared to the Waugh twins and I have no reservation in saying that, as a pair, they were better cricketers. Ian was the better batsman and bowlers preferred to bowl to Greg rather than to him. He was more difficult to dislodge. Steve Waugh has quality of obduracy, too, but I rate Ian as his superior.

We played New Zealand in our semi-final at the Oval, out-classing them and winning by five wickets with twenty-nine overs remaining. The Australians had to take on England in the other semi-final at Headingley. Conditions were such at Leeds that England's innings lasted only 36.2 overs and they were all out for 93. The amply built Gary Gilmour destroyed them with his six for 14 from his full quota of overs. Bowling a full length from over the wicket, his left-arm deliveries were often unplayable. That was the peak of his career and he only played in fifteen Tests. The pitch was the same one that had been used for the Pakistan v. Australia match ten days earlier and had been heavily watered. Once it dried out, the Australians should not have had too much difficulty in knocking off the runs, but they still lost six wickets before reaching their target. I would have preferred England to have won, and they may well have done if Mike Denness had won the toss.

In the final at Lord's Ian Chappell won the toss and asked the West Indies to bat. At 50 for three Chappell thought his side was in with a good chance and the neutrals probably thought so as well. Roy Fredericks was desperately unlucky to brush his foot against the leg stump as he played a hook shot over the ropes. Clive Lloyd, playing some stunning shots, raced to his hundred as Rohan Kanhai, in his final match for the West Indies, held firm at the other end with an invaluable innings of 50. They put on 149 and virtually took the game out of the reach of the Australians. As Lloyd has pointed out, sides used faster bowlers almost exclusively in one-day matches at that time and that worked out in favour of the West Indies. In recent years captains have turned to slower bowlers in these matches, especially on the slower, lower pitches of India, Pakistan and Sri Lanka. Our total of 291 for six was a formidable one, even on a small ground like Lord's.

The profusion of run outs, three of them caused by Viv Richards, was an indication that the Australians felt the total was beyond them. Our bowlers, with Boyce again doing well with four wickets, kept to the off-stump line that Lloyd had insisted upon. At 233 for nine it was nearly all over and a dressing-room attendant arrived with a case of champagne. Remembering what happened in the group match when we had come back to beat Pakistan, I said 'Take it away, we haven't won yet.' Lillee and Thomson swung their bats and 41 more runs came as our fielding became a little slipshod. It ended when Thomson was run out and I gave the order for the champagne to be brought back. The players embraced and slapped each other on the back. It was an especially emotional moment for Kanhai. He was not in the original squad, being a late replacement for the injured Sobers, and Warwickshire had agreed to our request to release him.

Lillee and Thomson were more successful as batsmen than bowlers in that tournament but that did little to damage their reputation as one of the greatest and most feared bowling partnerships in the history of the game. Lillee had a beautiful action, swung the ball and had the hostility and bounce that distinguishes the best from the good. I had seen Thomson on a previous tour in Barbados, and when he bowled flat out there was no one quicker.

The final finished just before nine o'clock and it was as well it was a fine, clear beautiful summer's day. By the time we had collected the trophy from Prince Philip and received our four thousand-pound team prize, it was too late for a team celebration and most of the players, extremely tired but happy, went back to the hotel. We celebrated at an official team lunch the next day. The prizes, including the award to Clive Lloyd for Man of Match in recognition of his 102 in 108 minutes, went into the kitty and were shared among all the players. That is traditional in cricket.

Seven of the players from 1975 survived in the squad for the 1979 World Cup, which was also held in England. Kerry Packer's World Series had robbed most of the leading countries of their best players and there was speculation that the West Indian players who had signed for Packer, including Lloyd, would not be selected. I was a member of the selection panel that left them out of the tour of India and nominated Alvin Kallicharran as captain. At the annual meeting of the West Indies Board, a majority decision was taken to reinstate the World Series players and Lloyd was asked to make a token appearance for Guyana as a sign of good faith. The squad included four players who had not been signed by Packer – Kallicharran, Faoud Bacchus, Larry Gomes and Malcolm Marshall – and when the players met up I detected no coolness between the two sets of players. We were unified and I was very relieved. Bacchus, Gomes and Marshall did not make a single appearance but were cheerful and enthusiastic throughout.

Our bowling was stronger than it had been in 1975 with Michael Holding, Joel Garner and Colin Croft available. We had an easy draw with India, New Zealand and Sri Lanka in our group. The first match against Sri Lanka was washed out and we overwhelmed India by nine wickets at Edgbaston. Gordon Greenidge and Desmond Haynes put on 138 for the first wicket when chasing 190. Greenidge, who loved playing at Lord's, went on to score an unbeaten 106. Our third match, against New Zealand, was closer without the result ever being in doubt. The semi-final against Pakistan was the best game in the competition with Greenidge and Haynes posting another century opening stand in our total of 293. A dropped catch by Imran Khan at long-on when Haynes was 32 proved a costly mistake. When the free-scoring Pakistani batsman Majid, 81, and Zaheer, 93, were together, Asif Iqbal's side still had a chance of winning, but at tea Lloyd spoke to his bowlers and convinced them to bowl a leg-stump line to restrict them. It worked and both players fell to Croft.

England beat New Zealand in the other semi-final and we were confident of a second World Cup triumph in front of another capacity crowd at cricket's headquarters. In the absence of Bob Willis the England camp went for caution, which seems to be one of the characteristics of English cricket, and preferred an extra batsman, Wayne Larkins, to a specialist fifth bowler, which meant that twelve overs had to be shared by three part-time bowlers – Larkins, Geoff Boycott and Graham Gooch.

At 99 for four with Lloyd out, we were hardly in a good position. Then the remarkable Collis King, a Bajan all-rounder of tremendous energy and with a great eye, changed all that, bludgeoning 86 out of a stand of 139 with Viv Richards in only seventy-seven minutes. It was one of the best innings of its kind I have witnessed in a one-day game. To outscore Viv in their partnership was an amazing achievement. Viv's unbeaten 138 lasted three and a half hours and deservedly won him the Man of the Match award. Our total of 286 for nine meant England had to score at almost five an over and with openers Boycott and skipper Mike Brearley failing to push the score along as the situation demanded, there was little doubt about the outome. Boycott took seventeen overs to reach double figures and when Brearley was out for 64, 158 was needed from the final twenty-five overs. Against bowlers of the calibre of Roberts, Holding, Croft and Garner it was an impossibility. Maybe a few Collis Kings might have succeeded.

Collis, who enjoys life, is still playing good-class club cricket in York and continues to score quick centuries. He is a great enthusiast for the game.

Most of the 1979 squad survived for the third World Cup, again held in England, in 1983. This time, though, the Indians proved to be an insuperable obstacle. The warning was obvious when we lost to them by 34 runs in a group match at Old Trafford, although that result was reversed in a second meeting at the Oval. The competition had been extended with each side playing the others in its group twice.

An Australian side captained by Kim Hughes was beaten twice by us and we were firm favourites to win the final against India. It proved to be an undistinguished affair, the West Indies totalling a dismal 140 in fifty-two overs in reply to India's similarly uninspiring 183 off fifty-four overs. I was present and I had the feeling the spectators were a little short-changed that day.

I was back as manager for the 1987 World Cup, which was held in India and Pakistan. It was the first time the competition was held outside England and was acknowledged as a huge success, with large crowds, some exciting finishes and a lot of travelling.

Recognizing that the West Indies were lacking the bowling strength of previous World Cups, I tried to persuade Joel Garner to postpone his retirement. I begged him to come with us but he refused. The fast bowlers were Patrick Patterson, Courtney Walsh and Winston Benjamin. The back-up bowlers were Roger Harper, Carl Hooper and Viv Richards. It was not a powerful attack by any means and when England required 35 from their last three overs in our opening match in Gujranwala they got them. Walsh went for 14 in the final over, and I was extremely upset. England had needed 91 from the last ten overs with six wickets down and only one recognized batsman, Allan Lamb, at the crease. Lamb, who finished with 67 not out, was masterful in these one-day situations.

Worse was to follow for Walsh in the next match against Pakistan in Lahore. This time 14 runs were again needed off the final over bowled by the Jamaican, and the Pakistani last-wicket pair of Abdul Qadir and Salem Jaffer were in the middle, cheered on by fifty thousand wildly excited home supporters. Walsh went for 1, 1, 2, 6, 2, 2 and we had lost a second game we should have won, by one wicket.

We managed to beat Sri Lanka by 25 runs in Kanpur, only to lose again to England, in Jaipur, by 34 runs. Indifferent bowling was to blame. Both Patterson and Benjamin were erratic in their opening overs and Graham Gooch was able to hold the England innings together with 92 off 137 balls. Our new skipper Richie Richardson responded with a similar performance, scoring one more run, but the rest of the middle order failed him. Before the match a leading Pakistani official had asked me, 'Who are you playing in the next game?' When I told him it was England, he said, 'Who are the umpires? I can speak to them on your behalf.' I did not tell him! We succeeded in beating Pakistan in Karachi in a match marred by crowd trouble. Police had running battles with students and tear gas drifted across the pitch at one point. Richardson's 110 was his highest one-day score up to then.

To the disappointment of supporters of both host nations, the final was between Australia and England and seventy thousand people in Eden Park, Calcutta, watched the Australians win a narrow victory by 7 runs.

14 *Grovel*

I doubt whether any word used in a cricketing context has ever caused a bigger stir than 'grovel'. Tony Greig, the England captain, was a straight-talking man but his choice of that word when asked in a BBC interview what the home side would do with the West Indies in the 1976 series in England caused immense repercussions and had a telling effect on the outcome of the series. 'We'll make them grovel,' Greig said.

Did he know what he was saying? The dictionary gives the definition of grovel as to 'lie prone in abject humility'. To say that about West Indians, some of whose countries had only recently become independent of Britain, whose ancestors were slaves taken to the Caribbean from Africa, was an incredible gaffe that he must have regretted later. It provided our players with the best possible motivation. What incensed them even more was that Greig, although qualified to play for England through his parentage, was born in South Africa, brought up there and spoke with a South African accent. At the time South Africa was banned from membership of the ICC because of its hated policy of apartheid.

I did not hear the interview myself but some of the players did and they were very angry. English officials were embarrassed by it. Clive Lloyd was in his early days as captain and he was to say later, 'We resolved to show Greig and everyone else that the days for grovelling were over.' He was still very inexperienced as a captain and needed guidance, which I was happy to give. His career had suffered a setback on the 1975–6 tour of Australia when a powerful Australian team that included the Chappell brothers, Dennis Lillee, Jeff Thomson and Rodney Marsh won the series 4–1. I believe Clive learned many lessons from that experience that were the basis of his subsequent success.

I think the players, including Clive, on the England tour had respect for my knowledge of the game and I was able to help them. Not that they needed too much assistance because it was a strong side, with Viv Richards scoring 829 runs for an average of 118.42, Gordon Greenidge beginning to develop into a great Test opener with 592 runs, and two feared opening bowlers in Michael Holding, who captured twenty-eight wickets at only 12.71 apiece and Andy Roberts, with the same number of wickets at 19.17. Richards, Greenidge and Holding were all Cricketers of the Year in *Wisden* the following season as a result of their efforts.

All three were part of a new generation of West Indian players. The passing of the old guard had been signalled a few months earlier, before the start of the home series against India, when the Board had been faced with a dilemma about Lance Gibbs. He was forty, and although he had just broken Fred Trueman's world record of 307 Test wickets, we had reluctantly come to the conclusion that we had to look to someone else. The Bajan Albert Padmore, David Holford, Raphick Jumadeen and Inshan Ali were all tried in that series against India.

At that time I wondered whether all the criticism that a selector inevitably faces was worth the bother. I was unpaid, after all, and I still am in my current administrative position. I told the players I would be retiring as a selector, but several approached me afterwards and said, 'Manage, we would like you to stay on. We have confidence that you will pick the best side.' Such players as Viv Richards, Malcolm Marshall and Michael Holding offered their support. It meant a great deal to me and I stayed on.

One of the early highlights of the tour in England was when

Roberts bowled Greig for a duck in the first Test at Trent Bridge. If it was not the fastest delivery Andy ever bowled, it was close to it. Greig's off stump was sent cartwheeling back several yards. Just how much the West Indian fast bowlers had been motivated by his comments was shown in his low tally of 38 runs in his first five innings in the series before he found some form in the fourth Test at Headingley. He scored 116 and 76 not out in that match.

It never bothered me that Greig and a number of cricketers born in South Africa played for England. If they had English parentage, or qualified by residence under the laws laid down by the TCCB in England at the time, I had no quarrel with that. So many cricketers come to play in England that it is like the United Nations of the game. They have helped to improve standards there. If they hadn't, there would have been something drastically wrong with the English cricketers: they were bound to learn from watching these great players at close hand.

I always had a good relationship with Tony Greig, often ribbing him about his being a businessman. Everywhere he went he turned up with a briefcase. He was always looking for some way to cash in on things and it was no surprise that he played such a prominent role in the Packer affair. He was a strong-minded character and showed he was destined to be England captain by the way he controlled events on the 1974 England tour of the West Indies. Mike Denness was the captain, but Greig was pulling the strings. I never rated Greig a particularly outstanding Test player, though. He won a match for England bowling off-cutters in Port of Spain, taking thirteen wickets, and played a number of valuable innings but he was a useful cricketer, not a great one.

Mike Brearley made his debut in that Trent Bridge match, starting off with a duck. He was a very thoughtful player and a very good tactician and captain, but I did not think he was that good a batsman.

Greig was involved in another controversy at Lord's when Holding bowled a beamer at him and he had to duck to avoid it. At six feet seven inches that was not an easy thing for Greig to do. Holding apologized and said afterwards that the ball had slipped, he had not tried to bowl it deliberately. I was given a grilling by the English press and I remember John Thicknesse of the *Evening Standard* being particularly relentless in his questioning.

That was the summer when the fairness of the West Indian fast bowlers Holding, Roberts and Wayne Daniel was called into question. There was a great deal of criticism of the way they bowled short at England's veteran openers Brian Close and John Edrich at Old Trafford. I remember I was interrogated at length about that as well. The journalists would not accept my contention that on a lively pitch the bowlers were entitled to bowl short occasionally and the use of the bouncer had not been overdone. Holding and Roberts were bowling a little short of a length and, with their pace on that fast pitch the ball was rising more than is usually the case in a Test match in England. It was not a deliberate tactic to bully the English pair. Close was forty-five and Edrich thirty-seven; their ages doubtless contributed to the criticism. But England's selectors had picked them because of their ability to play quick bowling. You cannot think of a batsman's age when you are playing against him in a Test match.

The Australian umpire Bill Alley warned Holding for delivering too many short balls under the Laws concerning intimidatory bowling, and Holding was careful not to infringe again. Both Clive Lloyd and I agreed that Holding and Roberts had not bowled well. If they had pitched the ball up more they would have taken wickets. 'They got carried away,' explained Lloyd. They bowled much better in the rest of the match, finishing with sixteen wickets between them. Roberts would have had a hat trick if Greenidge, normally a sound catcher in the slips, had held an easy catch off the future *Guardian* cricket correspondent Mike Selvey. It was the second opportunity Roberts had of taking a hat trick in the match and each time he was unsuccessful. Lancashire's Frank Hayes was the batsman who thwarted him in the first innings.

Viv Richards was twenty-four that year and in his prime. His 232 at Trent Bridge was a classic Richards innings, yet he surpassed it in the final Test at the Oval when he made his highest Test score of 291. England's response at Nottingham was led by the Northants batsman David Steele, who earned the reputation of being a courageous battler against fast bowling during his innings of 106. The grey-haired Steele became something of an institution that long, hot summer, but much as I admired his gutsy performances, I could not really see him as a Test player. He was a good county cricketer.

I will always remember a shot played by Viv Richards in the Trent Bridge match. The bowler was John Snow and the delivery could only have been four or five inches short of a length. Viv pulled it in front of square on the legside and it flew to the boundary like a bullet from a gun. That is the kind of shot which distinguishes a great player from an ordinary player.

Viv always had a smile and was easygoing. But he hated losing and would sometimes get worked up if he didn't think enough was being done to stop the opposition coming out on top. As the successor to Clive Lloyd as captain he led by example and did a good job. He had one or two scrapes off the field and there were occasions when I had to cover for him. One was the celebrated occasion when he failed to come out with the rest of the team at the start of a day's play in a Test in Antigua because he had gone to the press box to remonstrate with an English journalist. James Lawton of the *Daily Express* had written a piece suggesting he had made a derogatory gesture the night before. Viv denied it and went to sort it out with Lawton. It was a major error of judgement on his part. No cricketer should seek a public argument with a journalist; it is always reported and pictures are published that do not reflect well on the cricketer. I was president of the Board at the time and asked him to apologize, which, to his credit, he did.

He was equally at fault when he had a row with Bobby Simpson, the Australian coach in a series in the Caribbean in 1991. Some strong words were exchanged. Both men believe in frank talking and it became very heated. Col Egar, the former umpire, was the Australian manager at the time and he asked what action was going to be taken against Richards. I spoke to Viv and after a short time he agreed to write a letter of apology, which ended the affair. Some of my colleagues in the Board wanted tougher action but I persuaded them that an apology was sufficient.

I liked Viv and got on well with him right up to the end of his Test career in 1991, when he seemed to blame me for contributing to his retirement. After his last appearance at the Oval, his 121st Test appearance and his fiftieth as captain, he stood and waved to the crowd when he came off the field at the end and was quoted as saying he was retiring as captain. I spoke to him subsequently and suggested he put that in writing. With the World Cup coming up we had to be looking to the future. He didn't tell me he wanted to carry on, and Richie Richardson was appointed to lead the side in the World Cup.

Viv was one of my favourite players. He was always in control, and always dominated the bowlers. Andy Roberts was the first great Antiguan bowler, and Viv was the first great Antiguan batsman. He is now coaching in Brunei and I look forward to seeing that country produce some good batsman as a result of his work.

Injury prevented him playing at Lord's in 1976, otherwise he might well have topped 1000 runs in the series. Larry Gomes, the Trinidadian left-hander, took his place. During the Test at Lord's the former president of the West Indies Board, Sir Errol Dos Santos, said, 'I think the captain and manager are making a mistake sending in Gomes at three.' I replied, 'Sir Errol, Larry Gomes bats three for Trinidad and I think very highly of the Trinidad cricketing administration, so who are we to send him in any lower?' Larry's unbeaten 101 in the match against MCC that preceded the Lord's Test seemed to indicate that he was a worthy number three, but, unfortunately, Sir Errol's prediction came true and he failed in the Test match itself. However, he had a successful tour, scoring 1392 runs for an average of 48, and was later signed to play county cricket for Middlesex. Less gifted than the present left-hander in the side, Shrivnarine Chanderpaul, Larry was the grafting type of player the side needed on occasions. Wayne Daniel, from that touring party, also went on to play for Middlesex and did well. He may not have been so effective in county cricket because they tried to correct his open-chested action and that cost him a little pace.

The selection of Gordon Greenidge for the tour was not received with too much enthusiasm at the time, but the Hampshire opener proved a good pick, averaging 65 from 592 runs and taking part in three successive opening stands of 116, 192 and 180 with Roy Fredericks in the last three Tests. Gordon seemed to like Lord's. His 214 not out there in 1984, which I watched in my capacity as president of the Board, was one of the most dominant innings ever played at cricket's headquarters by an opener and enabled the West Indies to record a great victory. They required 342 in five and a half hours and won with eleven overs of the last twenty unused. Greenidge and Gomes shared an unbroken stand of 287. It is the highest total ever recorded to win a Test on the final day.

Greenidge was a top-class player with a sound technique and a merciless approach to batting. His partnership with Fredericks was one of the finest in West Indian cricket and it was only surpassed by his link-up with Desmond Haynes later. I doubt if there has been a better pair of openers for the West Indies.

When I was in Bangladesh for the Wills Tournament in 1998 Gordon was working as a coach to the cricket association there and was highly regarded following his success in the ICC Trophy. He was made a citizen of Bangladesh following that triumph. Haynes was the much more jovial of the two, a good team man who was always ready with a smile and a joke. Although Gordon was the serious one, Haynes's career had a sad end when he sued the Board after being left out of an Australian series. He had been disqualified because he had not taken part in the requisite number of Red Stripe matches in the West Indies.

The Jamaican Lawrence Rowe played in two matches in the 1976 tour but was rarely fully fit for action. He had problems with sinuses and when we took him to a specialist for tests the verdict was that he was allergic to grass and wool, both elements that cricketers are constantly exposed to in their lives, especially in England. He was put on medication and just when he appeared to be making good progress he slipped getting out of the bath and injured himself. He was upset when we gave him a deadline for getting fit and it was another wasted tour for him. A batsman who played in a similar style to Frank Worrell in some ways, he never scored the volume of runs outside the Caribbean that he made in home Tests. He had a lot of talent, not all of it realized.

There were two innovations on the tour: the use of the four-man fast-bowling attack and the new commercial awareness of players. On every tour I had made to England we received invitations from companies to attend functions and were given presents. The same happened in 1976 but one day the senior players said they did not want to attend any more of these functions unless they were paid. It was tiring and if they were going to attend, they wanted some reward. I must say this had not occurred to me. I thought it was a nice gesture by the various companies. The players thought they were being exploited, and

Above The Barbados team in 1942, when I made my Test debut on my sixteenth birthday. I am standing on the back row, far left.

Frank Worrell (standing, far right) and myself (front, left) before our world record stand in 1946.

Right My stand of 574 with Frank Worrell at Port of Spain in 1946 stood as a world record for the fourth wicket for a short time. My 314 remained my highest score.

The Three Ws taking time out (*left*) and travelling by ship to England (*right*).

Meeting King George VIth at Lord's in 1950. John Goddard is in the middle.

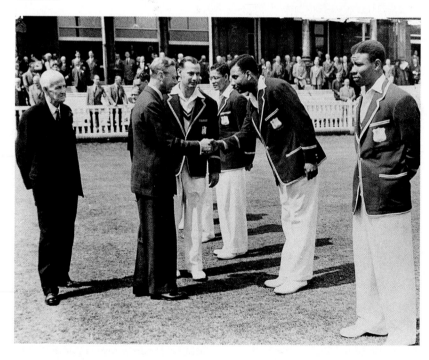

An attempted stumping off the bowling of Alf Valentine against
South Australia's Jack Wilson in 1951.

The West Indies team that faced England at Trinidad in the fourth Test
in 1954. Standing: Sonny Ramadhin, Bruce Pairaudeau, J. K. Holt,
Frank King, Denis Atkinson, Cliff McWatt and Wilf Ferguson. Sitting:
Clyde Walcott, Frank Worrell, Jeff Stollmeyer (captain), Harold Burnett
(manager) and Everton Weekes.

Left and above On my way to scoring 60 against E.W. Swanton's XI
at Eastbourne, April 1957; *Right* In action against England at
Edgbaston (all Hulton Getty).

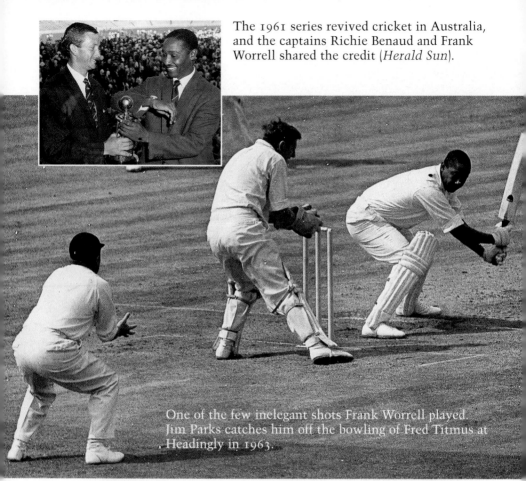

The 1961 series revived cricket in Australia, and the captains Richie Benaud and Frank Worrell shared the credit (*Herald Sun*).

One of the few inelegant shots Frank Worrell played. Jim Parks catches him off the bowling of Fred Titmus at Headingly in 1963.

Shaking hands with Her Majesty the Queen at Lord's in 1969. Prince Charles is on the left, and on my left is Peter Short, my assistant manager.

Manager of the West Indies side that won the first World Cup, in England in 1975. Standing: Gordon Greenidge, Alvin Kallicharran, Andy Roberts, Viv Richards, Keith Boyce, Vanburn Holder, Maurice Foster, Collis King, Bernard Julien. Sitting: Lance Gibbs, Deryk Murray, Clive Lloyd, Clyde Walcott, Rohan Kanhai, Roy Fredericks (Ken Kelley).

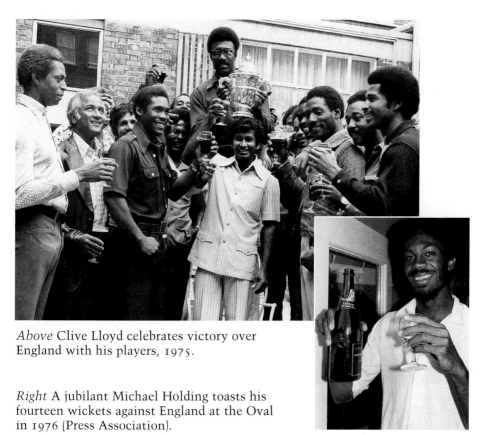

Above Clive Lloyd celebrates victory over England with his players, 1975.

Right A jubilant Michael Holding toasts his fourteen wickets against England at the Oval in 1976 (Press Association).

The greatest all rounders of them all? Keith Miller and Sir Gary Sobers.

The rulers of world cricket gather at the ICC conference at Lord's in 1996. I am in the middle of the front row.

Left Watching in South Africa with Dr Ali Bacher and President Nelson Mandela.
Right A recent photograph of myself and Everton Weekes.

maybe they were right. There is now big money in this sort of promotional work and agents are involved to see that the asking price is the right one.

We had two spinners, Albert Padmore and Raphick Jumadeen, in the squad and neither was really good enough to fill Lance Gibbs's position. The pitch for the first Test at Trent Bridge was hard and bare, and I thought it might turn for the spinners, so I advocated that we play one. Clive Lloyd and Deryk Murray, the vice-captain, disagreed, saying the quick bowlers would get more wickets at a lower cost. They were proved right and that was the first instance of a Test side using four fast bowlers, and alternating them through a day's play. The four in that Test were Roberts, Daniel, Bernard Julien and Vanburn Holder. Holding then came in at Lord's and stayed in the side. I made no apology for playing an unbalanced attack. You pick the best bowlers you have, whatever their pace. We were lucky we had so many outstanding fast bowlers coming along and the supply was unending for many years.

Tony Greig was back in the news in the fifth and final Test at the Oval. When Holding bowled him scores of jubilant West Indian supporters came on to the field to congratulate the popular young Jamaican and the umpires had to take the players off the field for a while. There was a great deal of criticism of the behaviour of these exuberant supporters and the TCCB later brought in ticketing arrangements that prevented large numbers of supporters of the visiting side sitting together. That was the start of the decline in West Indian attendance at Tests in England. The other deterrents for them were the high cost of the tickets and the sale of the tickets in advance, which seldom happened in the Caribbean. I do not condone pitch invasions but I felt the West Indians added a lot of colour and noise to these occasions.

Greig showed he had a good sense of humour when Holding finally captured his fourteenth wicket in that remarkable spell of bowling, and the West Indies won by an innings and 231 runs. As the players came off at the end he went towards the West Indies' section and fell to his knees to grovel to them. It was a delightful way to end a happy and rewarding series which brought pleasure to packed crowds.

15   *The Packer Affair*

I was a selector when the Kerry Packer affair erupted in 1977 with up to forty of the world's outstanding cricketers signing to play in World Series Cricket in Australia. Packer's motive was not to enhance the pay and conditions of cricketers. It was to force the Australian Cricket Board to sell him the TV rights to their matches. When they gave the contract to another company he decided to set up his own Supertest series. The news of the affair came as a shock to me. I had no inkling that anything like this was about to happen. Apparently, one of Packer's men had arrived at the Hilton Hotel in Port of Spain and had agreed three-year contracts with Clive Lloyd, Deryk Murray, who was secretary of the West Indies Players' Association and the man who negotiated players' contracts with the Board, and Viv Richards. Others were to follow.

Richards said he stood to gain seventy-five thousand pounds and the others were to receive much more than they could expect to earn in normal cricket. I think if I had been made a similar offer I would have accepted. As an amateur administrator and selector, it was my duty to help the Board solve a problem not of their making that would divide the West Indies team and the cricket-loving public. West Indies cricket had to look after itself.

Joey Carew was chairman of the West Indies selectors at the time, with John Holt and myself assisting him. The ICC had responded to the World Series threat by banning all the players who signed for Packer. He then sued the ICC for restraint of trade. As the ICC headquarters was at Lord's the case was heard in the High Court in London in front of Mr Justice Slade. The ICC lost. The verdict was such a damning one that Jack Bailey, in his capacity as secretary of the ICC, said there would be no appeal. The cricketing Boards had to pay more than two hundred thousand pounds in court costs, money the game could ill afford.

The cricketing nations were not totally unified over what to do with their Packer players. Australia insisted on a hard line and I remember speaking to some of their officials when an Australian side captained by Bobby Simpson, brought out of retirement after ten years, arrived in the Caribbean early in 1978 to play the West Indies. The Australians had chosen a new side, ignoring their Packer players, and they lost the opening two Tests by large margins.

The West Indies had taken a softer line and we selected our Packer players, with Clive Lloyd retained as captain, because they had always made themselves available for official matches. The news that three more West Indians, Desmond Haynes, Colin Croft and Richard Austin, had signed up with Packer brought matters to a head before the third Test in Georgetown. As a Board we needed assurances that all the players would be willing to tour in India and Sri Lanka later in the year. Their availability appeared to be in doubt. It was decided to relieve Deryk Murray of the vice-captaincy and impose a deadline of 23 March for the players to commit to the forthcoming tour.

When there was no definite response by that date the decision was taken to replace Austin, Haynes and Deryk Murray, with Larry Gomes, David Murray and Basil Williams for the third Test. Our decision caused a furore throughout the Caribbean. Packer flew to Barbados with his aides and invited the players he had recruited and their wives to join him at the Sandy Lane Hotel, the most exclusive hotel on the island. The radio phone-in programmes were filled with callers demanding the resignation of the selectors and the Board members, as were the letters pages of the newspapers. It was a very emotive issue. In reply, the Board said they had made every effort to accommodate the Packer players.

Clive Lloyd's response to our changing the side was to issue a statement announcing that he was resigning as West Indies captain after twenty-nine successive Tests, mainly winning ones, in charge. Inside a couple of days all the other Packer players also resigned.

Fears of unrest in the crowd following the withdrawal of Lloyd, a local player, fortunately proved groundless. We named another Guyanese, Alvin Kallicharran, as captain, which may have pacified public opinion a little, and the only other survivor from the opening two Tests was the offspinner Derek Parry. The Australians still had Jeff Thomson in their side after his decision not to join World Series Cricket and he captured four wickets in the West Indies' first innings of 205. Simpson showed that he still retained much of his old skill, going in at number six and scoring 67, his side's top score in the first innings, at the age of forty-three. Centuries from Williams and Gomes put the West Indies back in the game, only for the Australians to set a record total for a side batting last to secure the victory.

It was a fine game of cricket as was the fourth Test, which the West Indies won by 198 runs to regain the Sir Frank Worrell Trophy. The Board lost one hundred thousand pounds from the series and took the decision to ask the ICC to reopen negotiations with Packer. We heard that Deryk Murray was being asked to help World Series Cricket stage a series of Supertests in the Caribbean the following season.

Those matches subsequently took place with special committees set up to organize them. The public was unhappy about it, preferring to see the real West Indies side rather than Packer's, and there was bottle throwing in the Georgetown match and a similar incident in Barbados. One commentator said, 'Packer's matches will be remembered more for their violent crowd scenes than their cricket.' Australian skipper Ian Chappell was fined by a Georgetown magistrate for using insulting language towards a spectator. But most of the players were generally quite well received.

Attendances in the games in Australia in the first Packer season were abysmally low and it was only when the day–night games started that the figures climbed above the attendances in official Tests. The players had tremendous workloads imposed on them and I know they felt they had to work very hard both on and off the field to earn their money. By the 1978–9 season World Series Cricket was claiming that 730,000 spectators had watched eighty-five days of its matches while the series against England played by the weakened official Australian team lost an estimated half a million pounds.

The West Indies Board was forced to reach an accommodation with Packer. In return for sanctioning the World Series matches the Board was paid a rental fee for use of its grounds and a proportion of profits over a certain sum.

The whole affair petered out in April 1979, with World Series Cricket being disbanded when the Australian Board concluded a deal with Packer's Channel 9 for exclusive rights to Tests and other matches in Australia for the next ten years. Packer had won his battle and cricket was able to resume in the traditional way.

Looking back, I think there were many positive things to emerge from the Packer years. At long last the game's rulers came to grips with the commercial world and won improved new deals with sponsors and TV companies. In England the Test and County Cricket Board signed a contract worth one million pounds a year with Cornhill Insurance. That sponsorship deal is still running today. Packer also had a good effect on players, who were made to realize that if they were to earn more they had to become more professional in their outlook.

The playing changes that were introduced, such as day–night games, coloured clothing, white balls, black sightscreens and easier identification of players have almost all been adopted in Australia and the trend is being followed around the rest of the cricketing world. In many respects there is not much difference between World Series one-day cricket and the cricket being laid on in the 1999 World Cup in England.

The arguments between administrators and players did not damage our relationships permanently. I continued to get on well with Clive Lloyd and we worked closely together afterwards. It was messy at the time but good came out of it.

16 *Staying Fit on the 1980 Tour*

One of the many advantages West Indian cricket derived from the Kerry Packer series was the signing of the Australian Dennis Waight by the Board as the team's fitness trainer and physiotherapist. Waight had been employed to look after Clive Lloyd's players in the World Series matches and impressed everyone with his work. The players liked Waight in Australia and wanted him to stay on. More than twenty years later he is still working with the West Indies team, and still doing good work. He gets on extremely well with them and they never complain when he puts them through gruelling routines.

Staying fit in today's overworked conditions is not easy, especially for fast bowlers. Our leading fast bowlers have an incredible record of fitness, probably better than any other set of pace bowlers. Not many of them have needed back operations and most have been able to continue playing into their thirties. Something that has contributed to their longevity is their slightly open-chested action. Most of them were uncoached and bowled naturally with that action, which is not to be found in the MCC's coaching book. It is an action which places less strain on the back.

Playing county cricket was another plus for our cricketers. It meant that when they were selected for a tour at the end of the season in England they were match fit and ready for action. The opposite was true of the players coming from the Caribbean.

They were underprepared and took longer to acclimatize. County cricket is a finishing school for so many overseas players and its benefits have enabled several generations of West Indian players to become ever better. In my time it was not possible to play county cricket. We could only play in the Leagues in the North of England one day a week, with practice on week nights. It was a good experience and we were well paid but it did not measure up to county cricket.

When the squad was chosen for the 1980 tour of England four of the fast bowlers were playing county cricket: Malcolm Marshall, Joel Garner, Michael Holding and Colin Croft. Nearly all the players were living in England.

An innovation that year was that we had complimentary use of six Honda cars, and the English-based players used them to visit their families when they had time off. Within a week or two what seemed to be a good idea was causing all kinds of problems. Players kept losing the keys, and when they lent the cars to others no one seemed to know where they were. We have a phrase for this kind of thing in the Caribbean: mass confusion.

Obviously it is better if the players all travel together on the coach. It helps team spirit. But I had no objection to some of the senior players going off to visit their families. Nor did I object to having wives and families staying with the players in the team hotel when they were so inclined. I reckoned it made the players more contented and they performed better.

Cammie Smith, a member of the Barbados Board and an ex-player, was my assistant manager and what a fine job he did. Cammie mixed well and was popular with everyone. He is now an ICC referee, representing the West Indies on the panel alongside Jackie Hendriks. I was pleased to accept the Board's invitation to be in charge again. Clive Lloyd had matured as a captain and I played a much reduced role on the cricketing side. With such an impressive battery of fast bowlers, great batsmen like Viv

Richards and Clive Lloyd in their prime and one of the greatest opening partnerships of all time in Gordon Greenidge and Desmond Haynes, we were well equipped to continue our record of success in England. For the first time in my travels to England it turned out to be a wet summer and that prevented us winning more than one Test. The other four were drawn.

The West Indies had just completed a miserable tour of New Zealand and we were relieved to be playing in our second home, England. The tour of New Zealand was notorious for a number of incidents, including the kicking over of the stumps by an angry Michael Holding and the deliberate act of running into an umpire by Colin Croft. The frustrations of the West Indies players were such that they decided to come home and the manager, Willie Rodriguez, supported them. Fortunately, good sense prevailed and they saw out the tour. The only person to suffer was Rodriguez. Now a respected administrator who has done sterling work in his native Trinidad, he was never invited to manage another touring side. As far as I know, none of the players was punished or docked any of his fees. That would not have been the case today.

In England a company put up a prize of a hundred thousand pounds if we won all eleven of our matches against the counties, and the players were keen to have a go. Marshall set the tone when he dismissed both Worcestershire openers Glenn Turner and Alan Ormrod in his first four deliveries at New Road. We won that match by seven wickets. Leicestershire were crushed by an innings and 21 runs and we made it three in a row by winning at Northants. The current chief executive of the English Cricket Board, Tim Lamb, was his side's best bowler, taking four for 73 with his medium-pacers. Derbyshire and Kent were also defeated to make it five on the trot. However, our fast bowlers could beat the county batsmen but not the weather. The sixth match, against Sussex at Hove, was drawn. That game gave me an opportunity to look at Imran Khan, the future captain of Pakistan. He made two classy fifties and seemed to be an all-rounder of the highest class. With the ball, Imran and the South African Garth Le Roux made a formidable opening attack.

Ian Botham was England's captain in the Tests and he had a poor series, averaging 18.77 with the bat and taking only thirteen wickets. For some reason Botham never performed well against the West Indies. He led by example and I thought his players respected him, but his problem was that he did not have a great side. He was overshadowed by his Somerset colleague Viv Richards, who had a richly rewarding series. Viv's aggregate of 829 runs in the 1976 tour had eclipsed my 827 against the Australians in 1955–6, and although he managed less than half that total in 1980 he still finished top of the batting averages.

The only result in the series came in the first Test at Trent Bridge, Lloyd's side scraping through by two wickets after Bob Willis was responsible for a middle-order collapse on the final day. Alan Knott and Bob Woolmer, both of whom had signed for Kerry Packer, were back in the England side, along with a third Kent player Chris Tavaré. Chris hardly played a shot in his two Tests and I cannot remember seeing a more defensive player. Woolmer was a well-organized batsman and was clearly a student of the game. He has become one of the leading coaches in world cricket, setting a lead to others in the sensible use of technology and playing a key role in South Africa's successful reintroduction into Test cricket.

David Gower was dropped after the Trent Bridge Test, which I felt was a mistake. He made 54 against us in the county match and struck me as a class player. I liked his footwork, which is the basis of batting success. Gower's was faultless, as was his timing. Too often England's selections are based on form rather than class and that is wrong.

Rain ruined the second Test but not before the 77,000 paying spectators saw three memorable hundreds: Graham Gooch's 123, Desmond Haynes's 184 and Viv's 145. Gooch's stance, with his bat raised high in the air, led our bowlers to think they could trap him with a yorker. We had some outstanding practitioners of the art of bowling yorkers in our side yet no one was able to beat him in that way. Mainly a front-foot player, Gooch scored relatively quickly without being adventurous. Desmond's innings was the highest score by a West Indian at Lord's. I was delighted to be one of the first to congratulate him, even though it was my 168 that formerly held the record. He was a very emotional cricketer. In a previous game after being dismissed cheaply he burst into tears in the dressing room. Later on, when he was given out at Kensington Oval in Barbados, he threw his bat outside the fielding circle. This time there was only joy and we all shared his pleasure. His partnership with Greenidge, who grew up in England and played for Hampshire for many years, was the most productive of any West Indies opening pair. Together they amassed 6483 runs in eighty-nine Tests with sixteen hundreds. Their average stand was 47.32, much lower than the 71 of Jeff Stollmeyer and Allan Rae, my contemporaries, but I have to say that Haynes and Greenidge were the better pair.

When we arrived at Old Trafford for the third Test we were greeted with headlines in the *Sun* newspaper about Greenidge's views on his fellow players and Lloyd as captain. It was the first part of a serialization of his book and his strongly worded opinions came as a shock to us. He said he thought Lloyd was unapproachable and I know Clive was upset about it. The players were naturally very angry, especially his roommate, who was also criticized. Gordon was something of a loner and didn't mix too well. He was on the moody side but everyone respected his ability as a cricketer. I know the newspaper had exploited the situation, publishing the material at the start of a vital Test and giving it lurid headlines, but Greenidge should have shown a greater sense of responsibility. He claimed what he said had been mis-represented and that he was going to have the book withdrawn from the shops. Of course, that did not happen. I understood that booksellers in the Caribbean, upset along with everyone else about the tone of the book, withdrew it from their shelves for him.

The turmoil had a more upsetting effect on Gordon than anyone else and he was out for a duck and 11, and also dropped a vital catch when Peter Willey was 13 near the end of the game. In a rain-affected match Clive Lloyd's 101 on his 'home' ground was certainly the highlight, but Willey's gutsy unbeaten 62 saved England from a second defeat. With his unusual stance, looking towards midwicket, Willey was certainly different. He was only an average player but I have been impressed with his umpiring. He is now one of the best in the world and is young enough to improve. As far as his batting style was concerned, though, I cannot see why batsmen think it is necessary to stand other than side on, looking straight down the pitch. However, in a recent West Indies side Clayton Lambert faced midwicket and I must say it seemed to work for him. On the subject of unorthodoxy, I cannot understand Alan Knott's current preoccupation with persuading the wicketkeepers he coaches, including Alec Stewart, to take up a position behind the stumps looking towards extra cover.

England had the Somerset captain Brian Rose in their side in 1980 and it was only the second time a county captain had played for England with a county colleague, in this case Ian Botham, acting as his captain. The only other occasion it happened was in 1937 when Gubby Allen was skipper and R. W. V. Robins was under him, both of them playing for Middlesex at the time.

Faoud Bacchas from Guyana was one of the newcomers in the West Indies side, and though he looked good in warm-up games he rarely succeeded in Tests. He was an excellent player of slow bowling and I believe he is still playing for the USA, a sign of his enthusiasm for the game.

It rained again in the Oval Test but that should not have prevented us from winning. A last-wicket stand of 117 between Willey, who made 100 not out, and Willis, with 24 not out, did that. The bookmakers made us short-priced favourites to win. We were handicapped by injuries to Croft and Garner, while Lloyd tore a hamstring chasing a legside hit. He had to hand over to his vice-captain Richards. Clive was so downhearted about it that he talked about retiring and handing over to Viv. I told him not even to think about it. 'The injury will soon heal and you will be back playing again and wanting to carry on,' I said. Viv said later that there was 'a conspiracy to stop me taking over as captain,' but I never heard of one.

Garner won the Man of the Series award, presented by John Arlott after the drawn final Test at Headingley. Again he was bothered by injury. England's Graham Dilley bowled at a lively pace in that match. He had a good-looking approach to the wicket and should really have had a longer career at the top. Injury forestalled him, as it has so many promising English bowlers.

17 *Fast Bowlers and Helmets*

If I had to pick my number one fast bowler from all those I have managed or selected, I would have no hesitation in nominating Michael Holding, who emerged on the disastrous tour of Australia in 1975–6. The twenty-one-year-old Jamaican athlete was compared in pace to Australia's fastest bowler, Jeff Thomson, at that time. When tests were conducted Michael's fastest delivery was timed at 97 mph, slightly faster than Thomson's. Others might have bowled a little quicker on occasion, or bounced the ball more menacingly at the throat of batsmen but Holding embraced all the finest qualities needed to be a great fast bowler, including pace, accuracy, purity of action and a classically smooth run-up as smooth as the thoroughbreds that he loves to back. At his peak he was consistently the quickest, and, as he showed at the Oval in 1976 when I was the manager, he could sustain that pace over long periods, even when operating on good batting surfaces that offered him no assistance. He took fourteen wickets in that match for 149 runs and was devastating.

I have known Michael for a number of years and admire him for his courtesy, his good manners and the smiling way he acts as an ambassador for the West Indian way of life in his role as an international TV commentator. With his arrival in the early 1970s a crop of tall, dynamic fast bowlers suddenly emerged who enabled the West Indies to dominate world cricket for about fifteen years, the longest period of supremacy ever enjoyed by one country. Just how this happened, I am not sure. It was not as if West Indians suddenly started increasing in height; the side has always boasted tall players.

Before the 1970s many Test matches had been won by a pair of fast bowlers, Lindwall and Miller for Australia, Statham and Trueman for England, and Hall and Griffith for the West Indies. Now there was a new phenomenon: four giant fast bowlers – Holding, Andy Roberts, Joel Garner and Colin Croft – all playing in the same side. There was no escape for the batsmen. These bowlers changed the game, and the other Test-playing countries started to field sides with four quick bowlers. But they were not as quick or as dangerous as Clive Lloyd's quartet.

In the group I class as the greatest of my time I would include Roberts, Wes Hall, Malcolm Marshall and Curtly Ambrose. There is very little to choose between them but I vote for Marshall as the number two behind Holding. His total of 376 Test wickets for the West Indies has now been overtaken by Courtney Walsh but that is immaterial. Marshall had so much control even when swinging the ball at speed that he reigned for more than twelve years in Test cricket. Not many people will remember him bowling a bad ball in that time. He attended the same school, St Giles's Boys School in St Michael, Barbados, as Wes Hall but, unlike Wes, started out as, in his own words, 'a gentle medium-pacer'. He soon speeded up to become one of his country's fastest and most reliable bowlers. Playing as a professional for Hampshire at Southampton on one of the flattest pitches in the English county championship undoubtedly helped him master all the arts of fast bowling.

No batsman relishes playing against genuine pace, especially the type of bowling that comes at your midriff. I am no different. I would not be afraid to play against any of them but it would be an experience to be endured rather than enjoyed.

That would certainly apply to the prospect of facing Ambrose, the six-foot-seven-inch-tall Antiguan whose career continues to defy all the odds. He was a late developer, having been a basketball player earlier in life, and I remember being impressed with him when I was a selector. I advised the other selectors to have a look at him and they were also impressed. It was not long before he was playing Test cricket. In those days he bowled an exceptionally good yorker that earned him many of his wickets. He seems to have lost that in recent years but he still retains the ability to bowl straight and get the ball up to shoulder height, which makes playing shots very difficult.

I include Andy Roberts, another Antiguan, in my top group because he made the batsman play all the time, and was fast and aggressive with it. He had a mean, broody look about him, just like Ambrose, which doesn't improve the confidence of the batsman. He, too, was a late starter, playing his first game of cricket after he left school at sixteen. *Wisden* once claimed that 'his bowling stirs the blood' and it often spilled the blood as well, as a number of his victims can testify, including Steve Camacho and Ian Botham.

The other bowler in my top five is Wes Hall, who has been a friend of mine for many years. With his gold chain flying in the air and his arms whirling away, he was a fearsome sight: fast, hostile and always challenging. He also swung the ball away. Wes was renowned for being absent-minded, a reputation that was only enhanced by his self-deprecating stories. Once he hired a Holden car in Australia to take him to the races, but forgot the licence number. When he came out after the racing was over the car park was full of Holdens and he was extremely perplexed. Which one was his? He had to wait until the next to last car had left before he was able to drive off. On another occasion I remember him taking his cricket bag to his car, putting it on the ground, opening the boot while talking to colleagues, then proceeding to close the boot, get into the car and driving off, leaving the bag still on the ground. He was a great cricketer and a jovial, friendly man. He eventually went into politics and was the Bajan Minister of Tourism until he resigned after a disagreement with the Prime Minister. He has now become a clergyman.

Wes's partnership with Charlie Griffith in the 1960s was lethal and one of the main reasons why the West Indies were able to do so well against England in that period. I put Charlie in my second group of fast bowlers. He had a comparatively short spell as a Test cricketer, which was a little surprising in view of the way he looked after his body. He could be moody and that might have been held against him by some people of influence. He bowled a dangerous yorker and some of his opponents, notably the Surrey and England batsman Ken Barrington, thought he threw that particular delivery and maybe one or two others besides. The West Indians were divided on the issue. Those who played with him said there was nothing wrong with his action, but opponents were sceptical. He was eventually no-balled for throwing in England. Since his premature retirement from the top level he has devoted a great deal of time to cricket administration.

Colin Croft joins Charlie in my second group because he was quick and had a strike rate that was superior to many. He bowled from wide of the crease, moving the ball into the batsman and was capable of bowling for long spells. As the fourth member of the great 1970s quartet he probably benefited from the work of his colleagues, who had usually softened up the batsmen before he came on. These days he is a commentator and writer on the game.

One other bowler deserves consideration. Sylvester Clarke, the Bajan who appeared in eleven Tests, and who once was involved in a controversial incident on a tour of Pakistan when he threw a brick back into the crowd, was capable of bowling extremely fast and commanded a great deal of respect, especially on the English county scene. However, he did not maintain the necessary level of fitness and his bowling suffered. All of the truly great bowlers I have mentioned worked very hard on their fitness and stayed in good condition. Many fast bowlers from other countries seem to break down, especially with back trouble. The West Indians are, in the main, exceptions to the rule. Courtney Walsh is certainly an outstanding example of a fast bowler who keeps going. At thirty-six he was still taking wickets in South Africa in 1988 on the first tour by a West Indian side to the new republic after a long season in England. Like Ambrose, he has the appearance of an automaton, a bowler who can drop every delivery on the target area. Sir Richard Hadlee's world record is within his grasp.

Barbados and Jamaica are the two countries that have provided the West Indies with most of their quick bowlers. This is partly because there are firm, reasonably bouncy pitches in these islands that give the fast bowlers help. The pitches in Guyana, Trinidad, Antigua and the other islands have less bounce and are more helpful to the spinners, particularly in Trinidad.

The West Indies are constantly searching for heirs to the Holding–Marshall tradition. Nixon Mclean is the quickest of the new generation: he can get the ball into the ribcage area at a considerable pace but is still a little raw. Reon King, the Guyanese bowler who was in the most recent West Indies A team, is another young bowler of potential, along with Pedro Collins.

The best fast bowler I ever faced was Ray Lindwall. He was very quick through the air, moved the ball late and had a lethal bouncer. He had a low, slingly action that I found hard to counter. Others may have taken more than his 228 Test wickets in sixty-one matches but I know who I would least like to face. I much preferred facing his partner, Keith Miller, who had a high action that made it easier to pick up the line of the ball. It was similar with Freddie Trueman and Brian Statham. Trueman, with pace, aggression and an action that was similar to Lindwall's was a more difficult proposition. Then there was Frank Tyson, the man many experts rated as the fastest of them all. I played against him in Barbados when he appeared for Jim Swanton's touring side and I agree he was very quick. But he wasn't at his peak long enough to judge him against the best of the West Indians.

A question I am often asked is which fast bowler bowled the meanest, most dangerous bouncer. There are many candidates, most of them West Indian, but the two who stand out are Andy Roberts and Malcolm Marshall. Both of these great bowlers tended to skid their bouncer through, making it more difficult for the batsman to take evasive action. Roberts also bowled his at variable pace, and his strike rate of hitting batsmen was probably greater than any of his rivals. I hear that South Africa's Shaun Pollock is compiling a growing list of batsmen he has struck on the helmet.

I have always defended the right of the fast bowler to bowl bouncers. As long as these deliveries are used sparingly, as a surprise weapon, I have no problem with it. The bowler's intent is to keep the batsman more on the back foot, which gives him more chance of yorking him. I may be wrong, but I have the impression that the yorker is not used so much these days. Courtney Walsh and Curtly Ambrose are masters of it, but I would not put them in the same class as Joel Garner or Charlie Griffith.

Once a batsman reveals he is worried about short-pitched bowling he will get more of it, and then it is up to the umpire to rule whether it is intimidatory. The ones who are hit are those who do not go back and across, and that might be a legacy of one-day cricket.

In my long playing career I was never hit on the head while batting and nor were Everton Weekes or Frank Worrell. There were countless other batsmen who were not hit, including Sir Donald Bradman, Sir Gary Sobers and two Englishmen renowned for the way they played the hook shot, Reg Simpson and Colin Milburn. Yet today many leading batsmen are hit on the helmet at some stage in their careers. Why is this so? Maybe they take greater risks because, with the protection of the helmet and the visor, they know they are not going to be seriously hurt. Another reason may be that wearing a helmet, which weighs a few pounds, impedes the batsman's ability to get out of the way of the ball.

Players of my era moved quicker because they knew if they didn't, they stood a greater risk of being injured. Most West Indians play short bowling on the back foot, moving back and across, inside the line of the ball, which then passes them over the left shoulder. Many of today's players play off the front foot and it is more difficult to take evasive action when playing in that way.

An additional factor today is that there is much more quick bowling throughout the cricketing world. However, I doubt whether there are more bouncers bowled because the ICC has asked umpires to act against intimidatory bowling.

Viv Richards never wore a helmet, and in his book *Hitting Across the Line* he wrote,

I do not think that helmets have done anything to improve the game of cricket. They make it possible to play top-class cricket without fear and with the removal of that fear a certain amount of excitement has gone. There are some players, now international players, who would not be in cricket at all if it was not for the helmet. They would not have the stomach, the bottle.

Fast bowlers can still intimidate but the batsman is allowed to feel braver than he naturally is. I look at Bradman who never needed such equipment to face Larwood because he had total belief in his own ability. He would have been a lesser player had he used a helmet. I decided, for better or worse, I would be on my own out there. I would not hide behind anything.

I suppose if I was playing today I would go along with the trend and wear a helmet. But I do not think I could wear a visor. I would find it too distracting. When I batted, if I saw a hair or a piece of fuzz protruding from my cap I would immediately flick it away because it upset my concentration. How modern players cope with these plastic visors I simply do not know.

The English batsman Patsy Hendren was reckoned to be the first to wear a helmet, and there is a picture of him wearing some kind of protective device on his head while playing in the 1930s. Former England captain Mike Brearley used to wear a reinforced skullcap under his cap. The advent of the helmet really came about in the Kerry Packer era when there were so many fast bowlers playing in the World Series in Australia and there were fewer restrictions on the use of the short-pitched ball. Every batsman taking part wore one. It quickly spread throughout the game so that everyone wears one today, making it extremely difficult for spectators to identify the respective batsmen, particularly when they are the same height.

This is why the introduction of numbers for players in the 1999 World Cup has been welcomed, especially by viewers at home. This had to come, and I am a little surprised it has taken so long. Often the spectator at the ground cannot read the name on the player's back and this innovation will simplify things.

One of the reasons why I would not be too happy about wearing a helmet and a visor is the build up of heat around the head. What about the air-conditioned helmet? I am sure someone will invent one soon and it will become commonplace. Maybe the current lack of such a device explains why today's players are always asking for water to be brought out to them, slowing down the proceedings. In the West Indies we always had water breaks and they were as necessary then as they are today in temperatures of 80–90 degrees. However, some batsmen take it too far these days and the practice should be curbed. The ICC is right to remind players that drinks should not be taken outside the approved drinks breaks, especially if it leads to time-wasting.

Constantly sending for new gloves when the player's existing ones become sweat-stained is another annoying practice. I am loath to talk about 'in my day', but we couldn't afford more than one pair of gloves and had to make do with them. We were not so laden down as the present player. In my younger days we used to share our gear. I was playing Test cricket before I owned my first pair of pads. I never wore a thigh pad myself and nor did Sir Gary Sobers. I felt uncomfortable with it and I certainly would not have worn a chest protector or an arm guard. Boxes, or the so-called abdominal protector, was another matter entirely. Yes, we all wore those, for obvious reasons!

Ian Healy, the outstanding Australian wicketkeeper, has started the trend of wearing a helmet while keeping in certain conditions and I believe that others will copy him. When the ball is jumping out of the rough, keeping wicket is a dangerous occupation, more dangerous than batting. If the keeper is standing up, the ball can fly out of the bowlers' footmarks and cause a nasty injury.

Close fielders invariably now wear a helmet and shin-guards. In previous generations fielders stood further from the bat. If you look at pictures of top batsmen before and soon after the war you will see the fielders ten or more yards away at short leg. The practice of batsmen playing forward with their bat tucked behind their front leg has brought about the rise of the very close infielder. He is there for the nick on to the pad, the bat–pad catch, which causes the umpires so many problems. Just how much protection these fielders should be allowed to have is a point for discussion. It would be against the true spirit of the game to allow them to cover themselves with too much protection. In England last summer I was told about one county fielder who stood close on the legside with his legs protected by normal batting pads, which he wore under his trousers. They were the next step up from the shin-guards.

The colour of the ball being used has also come up in debate. A yellow ball has been used in some one-day games and a white ball in night matches. Personally, I feel red is the right colour and the one most easily picked out by the batsmen in Test cricket.

On my earlier tours of England most Test grounds did not have sightscreens. Perhaps the grounds were trying to pack a few extra customers in at the expense of the poor batsmen. Lord's caused particular problems and it was only after Colin Cowdrey had his arm broken in the 1963 Test there that the MCC installed movable screens in front of the pavilion. Grounds in the West Indies have always had screens, and though some of the sight-screens may not be made of the best materials, they make life easier for the batsmen.

I have no objections to coloured clothing. One of the reasons it was introduced in the Packer series was that the players felt the white ball used in night matches would not be easy to pick out against the white background of the players' flannels. Night cricket is here to stay and I regret that I have never been able to take part in a day–night match. The players seem to find no difficulty catching high balls against the glare of the floodlights. In most Test-playing countries night matches are usually well supported and they will remain part of those countries' cricketing culture.

I am not so sure that night cricket works in England. It remains light so late in the evenings there, until ten o'clock in the middle of summer, that the lights are only needed in the last hour or two of play. It is only later, well into August and September, when the weather starts deteriorating, that lights can be used more effectively.

In the West Indies one-day internationals are always played to full houses anyway. To play at night, therefore, would not affect the attendances. What it might do is attract a different type of audience. But it is expensive to install lights on a permanent basis and that will act as a deterrent in the West Indies.

Bats are expensive pieces of equipment and even in these more affluent times we have to be careful they are not priced out of the reach of ordinary young men. The bat with which I scored my highest score of 314 not out in 1946 had two straps across it, glued to the wood by the groundsman, to protect the cracks. There was a shortage of rubber after the war and the handle was encased in chamois leather held in place at the top and bottom by twine.

Traditionalists may not like it but there will continue to be innovations in cricket. The game has become more commercial and faces the problem of competing with other sports that perhaps appeal more to the young. However, cricket lovers like myself want to see the old values remaining. Sportsmanship and playing the game in the right spirit are as important now as at any time in the history of the game. When we adapt, as we must, to the changing times, we should not lose sight of that.

18 *The Best*

The biggest advance made in the game of cricket since I started playing the game in the 1930s has been in fielding. The South African Jonty Rhodes is by far the best fielder I have ever seen. In my day no one dived to stop the ball. Today almost all the players do, but none of them can match the agility and brilliance of Rhodes. He saves up to 30 runs an innings for his side and creates innumerable run outs that would be beyond the normal fielder. He has made an art of fielding and raised it to levels that youngsters will seek to emulate in the years to come. I am sure there are many young black cricketers in South Africa who will be aiming to be 'another Jonty Rhodes'. He has been a great ambassador for his sport and his country.

While the West Indies were world champions the catching was of the highest standard. Since then it has declined and I believe we lag behind some of the other countries in ground-fielding. West Indians are not often seen diving in the outfield like Jonty.

Of course there have been outstanding fielders in his position in previous generations and I think immediately of the Australian Neil Harvey and our own Clive Lloyd. Both were magnificent cover-points with tremendous throws. There were few better throwers in my time than Harvey.

As for slip catchers, my top three would be Everton Weekes, who was an exceptional fielder in any position but unrivalled in the slips, the former Australian captain and manager Bobby Simpson and Viv Richards. At the time of the West Indian supremacy throughout the 1970s and 1980s I cannnot remember Viv dropping too many chances. Catching most of the opportunities that came their way was one of the reasons why Lloyd's team was so successful.

The number one short-leg fielder I saw or played with has to be Gary Sobers. He usually fielded square or just behind square and his reflexes were amazing. He averaged more than a catch a Test; it was usually one of the highest class.

I damaged my throwing arm when still a schoolboy and was unable to throw any great distances thereafter. I took up wicket-keeping and later fielded in the slips. One long-throw expert who was outstanding in his era was the late Keith Boyce. He had a long, low throw from the boundary that powered the ball in to the keeper, almost like a baseball throw. Cricketers today play so much cricket that putting their shoulder out is becoming a regular occurrence. There are not so many good long throwers around, although I have to say not many fielders stand on the boundary rope these days.

I have played with and against, or watched at close hand, most of the leading captains of the past sixty years and the one who impressed me most was the Australian Lindsay Hassett, who followed Don Bradman as Australian captain. I played against him on one tour and found him a brilliant tactician. He was able to pinpoint the weaknesses of batsmen and asked his bowlers to exploit them. He was inspirational in his field placings. Two others worthy of mention were England's Peter May and Australia's Richie Benaud. As a thinker and student of the game, England's Mike Brearley commanded a lot of respect but his record was flattered by results against sides weakened by defections to Kerry Packer.

Fast bowlers abounded in my time in cricket and, as I mentioned earlier, Ray Lindwall was the best. He had a wonderful action, bowled with great pace and accuracy, tended to skid the ball through at batsmen and swung it as well. On top of that he bowled a lethal bouncer. In terms of pace and aggression Freddie Trueman was not far behind him. He also tended to skid the ball through and I always found that harder to contend with than the bowler who had a high action.

The best offspin bowlers I played with and against were Lance Gibbs and Jim Laker. Jim dismissed me thirteen times, as I have said, and his 193 wickets in only forty-six Tests cost just 21.24 apiece. He tended to have some help from the pitch at the Oval, and once on a celebrated occasion against the Australians at Old Trafford, but he also spent long days bowling on flat pitches abroad. When the pitch took spin he was the king.

Lance was the top offspin bowler on hard pitches. He had the longest fingers of any bowler I knew and would wrap them around the ball and give it a terrific tweak that would enable him to spin it on the most unresponsive of surfaces. He was the kind of competitor who always tried his hardest and never gave up. For that reason he never liked playing in charity matches. If they asked him to throw the ball up, he usually imparted so much more spin on it that the batsman was still in difficulty. An outspoken man at times, he didn't like shirkers and would make his views known. He had strong opinions on the game and was in many ways an ideal vice-captain for the West Indies. He liked an argument. In one match in Barbados when he was captain and I was manager he kept his slow bowlers on for more than 125 overs without making a change. At tea I suggested he should take the new ball but he was adamant that no change was necessary. We spent a long time that evening discussing it. Admittedly, his opening bowlers, both medium-pace, were not particularly impressive. Next day he used his opening bowlers and they took wickets. At lunch he still insisted he had done the right thing the day before. I was best man at his wedding and he is now a successful businessman in Miami. He also managed the West

Indies tour of England in 1991 and still comes to the Caribbean regularly to watch cricket ... and to have an argument.

The best legbreak and googly bowler I played against was the Indian Subhash Gupte, a big spinner of the ball who had tremendous variation. He also played in the Lancashire League when I was there and took a large number of wickets. I have seen Shane Warne on a number of occasions and without doubt he is the best of all time. He turns the ball more, and quicker, than any other legspinner. His success has revived one of the finest arts of all in cricket and cricket lovers should be grateful to him. I certainly am. He has brought me great pleasure watching him bowl.

There have been some great slow left-arm bowlers in my lifetime. Alf Valentine turned the ball more than any of his rivals, but in terms of all-round artistry and skill I would have to choose between two Indians of different generations: Vinoo Mankad and Bishen Bedi. Both were masters of flight and I give the edge to Mankad, whom I played against on a number of occasions. Mankad was also a top-class batsman. He would often open the innings for India.

Swing bowlers have won matches throughout the ages and there are a number of oustanding practitioners of the art around today, including the Pakistani pair Wasim Akram and Waqar Younis, both fast bowlers, and the South African Shaun Pollock. My nomination as the best of my time goes to Gary Sobers. He had no trouble swinging the ball while bowling in his faster mode and had the advantage of being able to swing the ball back into the right-handed batsman from the off as a variation to the one that swung away towards the slips. His most dangerous delivery was the one bowled from over the wicket that swung in and then left the batsman. Gary was a three-in-one bowler for the West Indies and I always felt he was at his most dangerous with the new ball when he was swinging it. Having watched the recent South Africa v. West Indies series in South Africa, I would consider the best pair of fast bowlers playing today to be Allan Donald and Shaun Pollock.

The finest opening batsman I played against was, without any doubt, Len Hutton. He fitted all the requirements of the opener and played some of his best innings when his side was under pressure against great bowlers. Geoff Boycott tried his best to emulate him and was a fine player. Hutton was a better one.

The opener I would select as my choice in the category of those I never played against picks himself, Sunil Gavaskar. He was very solid, dealt with fast bowling superbly and played shots, including the hook shot. Australia had no one in that class and the best of the West Indians, Gordon Greenidge, was a little way behind him.

My favourite left-handed batsman was Gary Sobers. He faces some strong competition, including Neil Harvey, Brian Lara and someone I never saw play, Graeme Pollock. There was also, of course, Clive Lloyd.

Sobers also tops the best all-rounder category. His game was literally all-round, fast, slow, back of the hand, orthodox, un-orthodox, outstanding fielding close to the wicket and batting of the very highest class, which made him the West Indies' most prolific scorer in Tests until he was overtaken by Viv Richards. I considered some great all-rounders – Keith Miller, Imran Khan, Ian Botham, Kapil Dev and Sir Richard Hadlee. None could compare with Sobers. Inevitably, that makes Gary my top crick-eter. Best all-rounder, best-left-hander and best swing bowler. Recently, he received a further honour when he was made a National Hero by the Bajan government. There are twelve Heroes, only two still living.

My selection of outstanding right-hander in my time is a choice between the other two Ws, Sir Frank Worrell and Sir Everton Weekes. Frank was sheer class, a player of elegance, with the confidence to improvise when necessary. I remember once we were playing for charity in Antigua before regional cricket came to that island; a local side bowled and fielded against us while we batted together for two hours. If we were dismissed it wouldn't have mattered but we were never got out. The object was to see us bat. A medium-pacer was bowling to Frank and, to my astonishment, he lifted his bat high towards cover as the ball was about to pass outside his leg stump and brought it down behind his back to hit the ball for a boundary towards square leg. I have never seen anyone do that before or since.

Everton's Test average was 58, nine higher than Frank's, and he also had a higher aggregate. I think that reflected the small difference between them. Everton was a player who could dominate throughout. He was equally good off both front and back foot and there wasn't a shot he couldn't play. I never saw him reverse sweep but no batsman of our time employed that shot. I am not in favour of it because it presents too many risks when set against the rewards it might bring.

That only leaves my top umpire. One stood out in his time, the years before the last war and immediately afterwards: Frank Chester. He was a reliable umpire who made few mistakes and enjoyed the company of cricketers. He had enough confidence in his ability to have done well in any era, even in today's highly charged atmosphere.

Umpiring is not a job I would have liked to have done myself. The only time I stood in a game, a charity event, I found myself appealing along with everyone else when a delivery struck the batsman's pad right in front of middle stump. I realized then that I did not have the right temperament for the job!

19 *South Africa*

John Arlott, the English writer and broadcaster, who was the voice of cricket, once went to South Africa during the apartheid years. When he arrived at immigration an official told him he had not fully completed his entry form. Opposite the word 'race', Arlott had left a blank space. 'I am a member of the human race,' he said with a contemptuous ring to his voice.

Arlott articulated so eloquently over the years what the rest of the cricketing world felt about apartheid, the so-called separate development of races introduced by the Nationalist Party of South Africa when they took office just after the last war. The world ruling body of cricket spent a great deal of time between 1970, when South Africa was barred from membership of the ICC, and 1992, when the new republic's newly formed United Cricket Board of South Africa was readmitted, discussing the issue. The West Indies were at the forefront of the countries who could not agree to any compromise until apartheid was finally ended. During those fraught years I had the feeling that some of the predominantly white countries would have done a deal if the politicians had allowed them to. That would have split the cricket world into two: the white countries of England, Australia, New Zealand and the white-dominated Board of South Africa playing among themselves and the non-white countries – the West Indies, India, Pakistan, Sri Lanka and Zimbabwe doing the same thing, with a catastrophic result for the game generally. That would have been a tragedy of the highest magnitude. Thankfully it never happened.

I never went to South Africa during apartheid for obvious reasons. But I have been there on four occasions since and have seen what dramatic changes have taken place. I will never forget the feelings I experienced when I was taken to a township for the first time in 1992. The place was called Alexandra and is near Johannesburg. It occupied a speck of land totalling just one square mile. Within its boundaries were 250,000 blacks. Barbados has roughly 260,000 people living in 166 square miles and we say it is overcrowded.

No one had to tell you that you were visiting an area that had been neglected and underfunded for decades. You could smell it. The stench of human waste was everywhere because there was no proper sewerage. I was horrified at what I saw. There was one football pitch. That was the only source of recreation available that I had seen. Now it has a cricket field as well, provided by the UCBSA's development programme. In townships all over South Africa young blacks are being coached and trained but, as expected, progress is slow. Before the series against the West Indies in 1998 various ministers expressed their disquiet that not a single black player was playing for South Africa at the start of the series. There had been one or two close to selection, but Hansie Cronje's side was an all-white one, drawn from Afrikaners like Cronje and players of English descent.

I met many people on my first visit to the country, which I undertook along with Steve Camacho of the West Indies Board. One was a white man who told me that he used to play cricket in Cape Town. 'One day we were playing a coloured side and the police came along and stopped the game, saying it was against the law,' he said. 'We abandoned it and went home, not wanting any trouble. A few weeks later we tried again and once more the police stopped the game and told us we would be arrested if we persisted. We didn't play any more matches because we didn't want to go to jail.'

Apartheid was said to be designed to discriminate against blacks. That was the popular conception of it in many parts of the world. But there were actually 117 laws in South Africa aimed at the Indian-descended population, the coloureds, as they were known. Basil D'Oliviera, a coloured South African, had fled the country to play his cricket in England. The man who made the transition possible for him was John Arlott. D'Oliviera was a role model in that era and his dignity won him great respect around the cricketing world. When he was chosen as a late replacement for the 1968 England tour of South Africa, South African Prime Minister John Vorster refused to let him back into his native country and the tour was called off. Fears of possible violence in England two years later caused the abandonment of the 1970 South Africa tour. The ICC excluded South Africa soon afterwards.

A total of seven rebel tours went to South Africa in the twenty years that followed, including a West Indian one captained by Lawrence Rowe. That brought no credit to anyone and it was the opposition in South Africa to the last of these tours, the one under the leadership of Mike Gatting, that forced a final change in the thinking of the South African cricket authorities in 1990. They decided that taking the game into the townships was a better way forward than bringing expensive mercenaries to their country.

Dr Ali Bacher, the managing director of the United Board, played a prominent role in the setting up of the development programme. In 1982, when he was chief executive of the Transvaal Cricket Union, he was jogging on the outfield at the Wanderers ground in Johannesburg and chatting with Alvin Kallicharran when Kalli started talking about beach cricket in the Caribbean. Bacher thought a kind of cricket along those lines might appeal to youngsters in the townships and found a sponsor to put up a modest sum to cover the costs. Lecgau Mathabathe, a Sowetan former headmaster who was detained during the 1976 student uprising, was a man with high-placed contacts within the African National Congress underground and he told Bacher, 'If the project is for the good of children, you will get our support.' The clinic was held in Rockville, Soweto, and is now the site of the Soweto Cricket Oval.

The cricketing authorities themselves were powerless to solve the South African problem. It had long been a political issue, with the United Nations drawing up a blacklist of those who had sporting links with the country. Similarly, the Gleneagles Agreement of 1977 specifically forbade contacts between the members of the Commonwealth and South Africa. We saw these charters being invoked during several England tours of the West Indies. On England's 1980–1 visit to the Caribbean the exact interpretation of the Gleneagles Agreement suddenly became a burning issue when the Surrey bowler Robin Jackman, who was one of fifty or more English county cricketers who made a living in the English winter by playing in South Africa, was called up as a replacement for Bob Willis. Jackman was not the only player in the England party who had played in South Africa – David Bairstow, the Yorkshire wicketkeeper who sadly ended his own life, was another.

Two days before the start of the Georgetown Test the British High Commissioner in Georgetown was told that Jackman's visitor's permit had been withdrawn. Within hours a joint statement was issued by Alan Smith, the tour manager, and the English Cricket Council in London that said England would not take part in the second Test because restrictions were being imposed on their side.

Alan Smith rang me to say, 'Robin Jackman has been refused entry to Guyana. May we come to Barbados. We want to come within twenty hours.' I rang Tom Adams, the Prime Minister of Barbados, and he said he was willing to allow it. He added, 'But whether Jackman can play is a different matter. I have to take notice of what my Caricom neighbours have to say on that one. I cannot act on my own.'

The England party flew to Barbados and a meeting took place at the Holiday Inn between representatives of the governments of Barbados, Montserrat, Antigua and Jamaica, the other islands where England were due to play. The talks were lengthy and it was 2 a.m. when Smith emerged from the Rear Admiral Suite at the end of the pier to tell the press that an agreement had been reached for the tour to continue.

The Barbados Test was played in an air of sadness because on the second evening England's assistant manager Ken Barrington collapsed and died of a heart attack at the team's hotel. This shattering event could well have taken place at my house. I had invited Ken and his wife Anne to attend a party but he said he had a prior dinner engagement of long standing and declined my invitation. He was a universally popular man who worried a great deal and I am sure that the Jackman affair caused him a lot of anguish.

On the next England tour five years later, the second successive 'blackwash' series, there was another disruptive intrusion of the South African issue when Graham Gooch took exception to comments made by Mr Lester Bird, Prime Minister of Antigua, and said he would not be going to Antigua for the final Test. The TCCB had to send Donald Carr out from London to persuade Gooch to continue with the tour, and Donald was eventually successful. Gooch played at the Recreation Ground and was out in both innings for the same score, 51, the same way, lbw, to the same bowler, Michael Holding.

I represented the West Indies at the ICC in 1988 when the subject of bringing the South Africans back into the fold was discussed at great length. Dr Bacher, Joe Pamensky and Geoff Dakin always turned up in London, and relations between the three were always good. We had to tell them that our position was exactly the same. As long as apartheid existed in their country we could never allow a West Indian side to visit and would not agree to the ICC changing its stance and letting any other side go there. We had little choice in the matter. Our governments would not countenance such a move. And as for rebel tours, I could not support any black man going to South Africa and being classed as an 'honorary white'. That was repugnant and dishonourable.

The players who went on these tours saw for themselves what the situation was like in a country where the people were divided into race and kept apart. One of them found himself being asked to leave a white section of a train and he did so.

The West Indies Board, in discussion with England and Australian Board representatives, reached a formula that they felt might be acceptable to all the governments. They didn't want world cricket to break up. We sounded out our various governments to try to find out if they could accept this formula. Allan Rae, the ex-President of the Board, met the Jamaican Prime Minister Michael Manley, Lance Murray met the Trinidadian Prime Minister and I met those from Guyana, the Leewards and Windwards and Barbados. The response from the governments was that any player who went to South Africa would be banned and there was no question of any tour, private or official, there being sanctioned. The ICC meeting took a long time to reach its decision because some countries felt cricketers should be able to go if they so desired and that to prevent them was restraint of trade.

Things were moving fast in the domestic politics of South Africa. President de Klerk's talks with the ANC were advancing rapidly and it was clear that, providing the white minority did not vote against the compromise plan that had been suggested, apartheid would soon be over.

The three key figures on the cricket side were Steve Tshwete, who was to become the Minister of Sport in the first black government, Krish Mackerdhuj, the first president of the UCBSA, and its indefatigable managing director Ali Bacher. When the ICC met again in 1991 formally to approve the UCBSA's application to join I felt the matter was being rushed and the Pakistani delegates felt the same way. Plans for the 1992 World Cup were well in hand and there was no provision for the entry of a team from South Africa. Eventually, though, the Pakistani delegation changed its stance and voted in favour. The West Indies' delegation was the only one to abstain. I told the others that it was too important a matter to approve in a matter of hours. And I had yet to discuss it fully with my Board members in the Caribbean. I felt I could not do that on the telephone. When the meeting was concluded, Ali Bacher said to me, 'Clyde, you are a statesman. You are looking at all the issues and I am aware of that.' I have always got on well with Ali, who was a gynaecologist before he became a cricket administrator. He is a tireless worker for the cause of South African cricket and world cricket generally.

Clive Rice, the forty-two-year-old all-rounder, was appointed the first captain of The Proteas, the name that replaced the old Springboks, for a symbolic short trip to India that preceded the 1992 World Cup. The South African squad was watched by hundreds of thousands of Indians as it made its way to Calcutta's city centre from the airport on 8 November and the euphoria was not lessened by two defeats in the three one-day matches.

Kepler Wessels took over from Rice as captain in the World Cup; the only non-white in his squad was the spin bowler Omar Henry. The South Africans beat Australia by nine wickets in their opening match to convince everyone that their twenty-one years of isolation had not unduly affected their cricketing prowess, and they went on to reach the semi-finals before losing to England in a match shortened by rain. South Africa needed 22 runs off thirteen balls when the umpires took the players off the field at Sydney. Within five minutes the weather had cleared but the rules of the competition were inflexible. The new target was a farcical 21 runs off a single delivery. The South Africans were out of the tournament and the cricketing world sympathized with them.

In April 1992 the South Africans journeyed to the West Indies for another symbolic trip. The West Indies won the three one-day matches with ease. It was a chastening experience for Kepler Wessels and his players, who had been so jubilant a few weeks earlier.

Phil Simmons, one of the best of the West Indian one-day players and probably the closest to being a one-day specialist, hit five sixes in his 122 off 109 balls in Kingston. When one of them went over the press box and into the street the boy who retrieved the ball insisted on free admittance before he handed it back. Apparently, this was not forthcoming so he ran off with the ball. The West Indies captain, Richie Richardson was booed by the locals in the same match. They thought he should have done better in the World Cup and were also unhappy that Jeff Dujon had been left out of the team.

The various regions of the Caribbean have always had an insular approach to the selection of the West Indies side and now we were to see one of the worst manifestations of it. Because of a boycott by the locals of the single Test in Barbados through the omission of the Bajan Anderson Cummins from the West Indies side, less than seven thousand people watched the five days of the inaugural Test. It was a depressing saga that brought only embarrassment and no credit to Barbados.

I thought the selectors were perfectly entitled to leave Cummins out of the single Test in Bridgetown. We had the vastly more experienced Curtly Ambrose and Courtney Walsh and they proved their worth when sharing all ten wickets in the second innings, thereby enabling the home side to make a remarkable recovery and win by 52 runs. Patrick Patterson and Kenny Benjamin supported them. In my capacity as chairman of the Board, the public wanted me to overrule the selectors and include Cummins. I was not empowered to do that and would not have done so anyway because I did not think Cummins was worth a pick. He was a moderate bowler, as his subsequent record has proved. An incredible cross-section of people who ought to have known better, including academics, politicians and journalists, supported the boycott. They seemed to think there were no justifiable cricketing reasons for excluding Cummins. I had to disagree. Jackie Hendriks was the chairman of selectors and when I spoke to him he said, 'There is nothing we can do. It's unfortunate.'

Nelson Mandela sent a telegram wishing all those involved in the match well and it turned out to be a fascinating Test match. When it started, there was hardly anyone in the ground and it was the same over the next four days. When the West Indies won there were barely more than five hundred people present. The West Indian players did a lap of honour, clasping hands, to show their solidarity.

After the match I heard that Brian Lara had been out with some of the South African players the night before at Harbour Lights, a well-known club in Barbados. When I saw Brian I said, 'I hear you are the person who should be man of the match.' He was a little surprised, and I went on, 'I hear you had the South Africans out until four in the morning.'

He laughed. 'Actually it was two o'clock, not four,' he said. He scored 17 and 64 and held five catches in the match. The Man of the Match award was shared by the South African opening batsman Andrew Hudson, who scored his maiden Test hundred –

153 in eight hours, forty minutes – and Curtly Ambrose, who took eight for 81.

Barbados was chosen as the venue because the West Indies Board felt it would make the most money. Gate receipts were minimal but the visit did not incur a loss for the Board as a South African company paid for the expenses of Wessels's team. Ironically, it was one of the few tours to the West Indies that resulted in a small profit.

I thought the South Africans showed their inexperience. They only needed 201 to win and at 122 for two at the start of the last day were in command. Walsh and Ambrose removed the last eight wickets for 26 runs in an inspired spell of bowling. They have been great servants of West Indian cricket.

The South Africans gave the appearance of having an inferiority complex. I do not think that is true now. Under Cronje, they have become a hardened, competitive side. Their officials tried hard to persuade us to have them back a year or two later but our schedule would not permit it. The tour came about through my visit to the new republic the year before.

I first met Nelson Mandela at the one-day series between South Africa, Pakistan and the West Indies on a subsequent visit. The day before he had been in long talks over the coming elections, and I said, 'I see you were having some problems yesterday.' He replied, 'Oh, yes, but all I really want to do is to get my people to forget the past and work together with all people for the present and future of our country.' For anyone who had been in jail for twenty-seven years to talk like that, with no trace of bitterness, was a sign that he is a great man. He looked tired, which was not surprising considering his workload and the pressures of bringing about change and reconciliation. He said, 'When I was in prison I used to train for two hours a day. Now I can only train one hour a day.' He did not seem to be too interested in the game, or to understand too much about it, but he recognized its importance in re-establishing his country as a sporting force.

He was presented to the teams and there was loud applause all around the ground and only a few boos. Ali Bacher was also given a great reception. He is one of those rare people who can remember a vast number of names. I was astonished when we went to watch some black cricketers being coached in a township and he addressed each one of them by his Christian name.

On my last two visits to South Africa I have seen the changes that are sweeping through society in this troubled land. However, the underlying divisions remain, as was illustrated for me the day I visited a shop in Cape Town to buy a flag as a souvenir for a friend in Barbados. The shopkeeper showed me some flags and when I asked if there were any others she handed me one with Nelson Mandela's picture on one side. I said, 'That's better.' She replied, 'Do you think so?' 'It's the new South African flag,' I said. 'Do you prefer the old one?' 'Yes,' she said. 'In the new South Africa the blacks are first, the whites second and the coloureds third. In the old South Africa, the whites were first, and the coloureds second. So we have dropped a place.'

During the visit of the South African team to Bridgetown for the inaugural Test the importance of the new flag was shown when it was discovered that we only had the old one to raise to the top of the flagpole on the pavilion. The South African management protested and in the absence of the new flag, none was hoisted. They explained that as the match was being shown on national TV it would not do to have the old flag flying.

20 *ICC*

I was a proud man when I was invited to succeed Sir Colin Cowdrey as chairman of the International Cricket Council in 1993. I became the first non-British chairman and the first black man to hold the post. The ICC has been the controlling body for world cricket for many years and it is only in recent times that it has assumed the powers to do the job properly. That process of reform is almost complete, and as we enter the new century I am confident that the ICC will be able to go forward and ensure that as many countries as possible are encouraged to develop the game. In 1997 Jagmohan Dalmiya of India was voted in as the first president in a new structure to serve a three-year term. Australia's Malcolm Gray will succeed him under the new rotational formula.

My role was changed to chairman of the cricket committee which is responsible for the Code of Conduct, standard playing conditions, the appointment of umpires and referees, the assessment of umpires, the organization of conferences for captains, umpires and referees and management issues of the World Cup, the ICC Trophy, the Youth World Cup and the general management of the game. I am unpaid, as are the other members of ICC who are not employed full time, and I consider it is an honour to serve the game that has brought me so much pleasure.

The ICC has attracted much criticism in the past and I believe a lot of it has stemmed from a basic misunderstanding of the role and powers of the organization. For example, we were criticized for not taking action over alleged match fixing. I had said on a number of occasions that I believed there was a case to answer, that with so much smoke billowing around there had to be a fire somewhere. But the ICC has no means of finding evidence, we do not employ detectives, and it was not possible for us to act under our rules at the time. The introduction of the Code of Conduct meant the member countries ceded power to us to punish on-field offences. It did not allow us to investigate matters that took place some time before, like an alleged bribery incident. In 1995, our powers were strengthened and in January 1999 we went a stage further. At last the ICC has decided to give the organization more teeth and has agreed to establish an ICC Code of Conduct Commission. This Commission will in future consider specific matters referred to it by the Executive Board, with particular regard to bribery and match fixing in international cricket. The Commission is to consist of three persons appointed by the ICC Board, one of whom will have a legal background. This is a step in the right direction, especially as the members of the Commission will be independent of any cricket board and will deal with serious disciplinary matters concerning umpires, team officials and administrators.

Bribery allegations, mainly concerning Pakistani players, began surfacing in the early 1990s but there was always insufficient evidence for the Pakistani authorities to act, until February 1995 when newspapers in Australia reported that Shane Warne, Mark Waugh and Tim May, secretary of the Australian Players' Association, alleged that the former Pakistan captain Salim Malik had approached them with offers of money to lose matches, including a one-day international in Colombo. Malik rejected the allegations.

In April 1995, Warne, Waugh and May signed sworn statements

that were forwarded to the ICC and to the Pakistani inquiry into the affair. The Australian Board said that their players would not go to Pakistan to appear in front of the inquiry. What wasn't disclosed at the time was that a year earlier Warne and Waugh had admitted to the Australian Board accepting money from an Indian bookmaker for giving information about the state of pitches and the weather prospects that would help him set his odds. The two players denied that they disclosed any other information and said they were paid a relatively small amount. Their Board fined them heavily. David Richards, the ICC chief executive, and myself were given this information by the Australian Board and told that they wanted it to remain confidential.

In October 1995, Malik was cleared by the Pakistani former Supreme Court Judge Fakharuddin Ebrahim, who claimed the conflicting evidence from May and Warne amounted to 'an unbelievable story'. The Australian Board rejected these findings and Malik left for Perth to join the Pakistan team. In November the Pakistan Board decided against launching a second inquiry. Meanwhile, there had been plenty of other stories about alleged match fixing, in Zimbabwe and in England. All sorts of illustrious names were dragged into the affair and they all denied involvement.

In September 1998 the Pakistan Board ruled that Malik, Wasim Akram and Ijaz Ahmed should not be picked for international cricket until further notice while inquiries were completed. It said five other Pakistan players should be investigated. The findings were forwarded to Lahore for a judicial inquiry. The story then became clouded when the ruling was ignored and Pakistan picked most of these players for the home Test series against Australia, which Mark Taylor's Australians won. They were the first Australian side to win there for thirty-nine years.

A month later, in October, Waugh and skipper Mark Taylor gave evidence to the inquiry in Lahore set up by the President of

Pakistan. Akram denied the allegations against him and skipper Aamir Sohail said he had refused bribes. At the end of the year the report of Judge Quayyum was handed over to the President's office. In Australia, Warne and Mark Waugh appeared at a press conference to admit that they had acted in a 'naïve and foolish manner'.

One of cricket's difficulties in unravelling this mess was that politics and cricket are inextricably intertwined in Pakistan and it is never easy to get to the truth of any matter. My view has always been that, with the necessary powers, the ICC should take a tough line and crack down on offenders if they are proven guilty. We have never had a major case of match fixing proved in cricket and the whole idea of it is repugnant.

One of the ICC's biggest successes has been the introduction of the Code of Conduct to halt declining standards of behaviour on the field. As the prizes grow bigger and the pressures on players increase, tempers can snap and I recognize that this is the way the game has gone. But we owe it to future generations to see that sportsmanship and fair play are upheld. The aim will always be to win, but to win with honour and dignity, and to lose in the same good spirit.

There is one overriding tenet in the Code of Conduct: namely, that the captain has responsibility for the conduct of his players. That is enshrined in the Laws of the game and the Test captains have accepted this responsibility in their conferences. The establishment of the match referee scheme was done to take pressure off the umpires, who told us they were becoming disillusioned with the way they reported incidents of indiscipline, mainly dissent, to the manager of the team concerned only to learn much later that no action had been taken. The umpires felt let down and we agreed with them. The ICC agreed to set up a panel of eighteen referees, two from each country, to monitor every Test match played. The referees, mainly ex-Test players, have powers to impose penalties on the spot. They sit in a small room next to a TV monitor and have access to all the replays so they can see an incident any number of times.

One of the referees, Ahmed Ebrahim of Zimbabwe, is a judge and won praise in England in 1998 with his three-page judgement over Allan Donald's infringement of the Code with criticism of umpires in a newspaper. The terms of reference of the cricketing 'judges' include adjudicating on breaches of the Code and imposing penalties for failing to maintain the minimum over rate, deliberate acts of unfair play and infringements of the regulation relating to advertising on clothing and equipment.

When the Code of Conduct was introduced in 1991–2 there were only four infringements by individual players. In 1997–8 the total had risen to twenty-two but this is because referees are becoming stricter rather than players becoming less disciplined.

I firmly believe that the introduction of the Code has resulted in a reduction in the number of unsporting incidents in international cricket, and that has to be welcomed. Although the level of sportsmanship in cricket has always been, and remains, high in comparison with other sports (ninety-five breaches of the Code by players in the first seven years is not, in my view, a worrying number when one considers the number of Test matches being played around the world) the game has still had its problems. The Australians started sledging, which is the use of abuse to unsettle an opponent. In my heyday they were all at it, Lindwall, Miller and others . . . there was hardly a player who did not sledge. Bobby Simpson, in spite of being the Australian captain and later a match referee, was never slow to make a few scathing comments when he thought it might unsettle an opponent and give his side an advantage. I never let it worry me. In fact, I cannot remember anything being said in my direction. They knew who to try out and who to ignore. Some players would react and let it get to them. Obviously, they were unwise to do so. There might have been some racist abuse, although I never came across an example of it.

I do not see the need for sledging. Nor do I see the need for bad language. It is virtually impossible to switch the television on these days without hearing swearing, often the 'f word', which was taboo for so long. Times change and so does language, but I still feel that coarse language is demeaning and undignified.

The Australians still lead the field in sledging, with England a close second. It has persisted as long as it has in the game because the umpires, though empowered to do so, hardly ever take any action. At a recent meeting of Test captains, they said they did not feel sledging was a serious problem, but if umpires considered it was, then they should inform the captains on the field, and they would speak to the players involved. Umpires have traditionally thought the best course of action was to report an incident to the match referee and for him to deal with it. They may still have to do this if there is no improvement after speaking to the captains.

Another abuse that the ICC is determined to curb is excessive appealing. The Indians and Pakistanis were leading culprits in the past but there were unwelcome signs that it had spread in the 1998 series between the West Indies and England. It became tiresome to see fielders constantly appealing when they knew that a batsman wasn't out. Usually it was for a bat–pad 'catch'. On more than one occasion a batsman could be seen with his bat raised high in the air, not playing a shot, when the ball bounced off his pad and there was nevertheless an appeal for a 'catch'. The sight of players charging down the pitch towards the umpire with arms raised, appealing for a decision was another unwelcome feature that has crept into the game. Particularly annoying was the way wicketkeepers led the charge. This was also discussed at recent conferences and I expect that some action will soon be taken against offenders. During one ICC conference with the umpires one leading official said the players were cheating because they knew they were appealing when the batsman was not out. They were seeking to get a wicket from a nervous umpire, panicking him into making a mistake in their favour. By and large I think the behaviour of the players in this matter has improved since the captains' meeting early in 1998.

Nowadays television highlights everything and the viewer at home can usually see if players are being dishonest. Players also know that if they misbehave, their actions can be caught on camera. It was reported that England captain Michael Atherton made a V sign in the direction of Philo Wallace in the Bridgetown Test in 1998. A cameraman at that end of the ground later produced photographic evidence to support the accusation.

I am not happy about the replaying of debatable incidents, particularly on the big screens at grounds. The big screen is used because it was said the viewer at home had the advantage of seeing replays so why shouldn't the spectator paying for his seat at the ground be given that same privilege? It also livened up the day. But it is a potential spur to crowd trouble and places an immense burden on the umpire, especially if the replay clearly shows that he has made a mistake. The TV viewer has the opportunity of watching several slow-motion replays before making his decision. The umpire has to make his mind up on one sighting, with no replays and no slow motion.

We have introduced the third umpire to look at replays over certain dismissals so that help can be provided to the umpires in the middle. This concerns line decisions, stumpings, run outs, hit-wicket incidents, boundary decisions and whether a catch has been cleanly caught if both umpires are undecided. The game has benefited from this innovation. With run outs and stumpings it is particularly difficult for the umpire to decide and the camera can help a great deal by showing things that are not visible to the naked eye. Problems still remain when the cameras are not positioned side on to the wicket, and there has to be uniformity on that issue in the near future.

However, I do not favour the extension of the use of technology to other decisions. The lbw decision can only really be decided by the umpire. The technology is not yet good enough to enable a third umpire to judge the height or the movement of the ball. Also, if we take too much responsibility away from the umpires, their authority is undermined.

The ICC has been hard on dissent, with the majority of the twenty-two breaches of the ICC Code of Conduct in 1997–8 being for this offence. It is said there is a fine line between dissent and disappointment. I maintain that a batsman knows when he has dissented. Referees have been swift to act and I do not believe dissent is as much of a problem as it was a few years ago. I sympathize with a young player starting his career when he is out to a doubtful decision. He may not be picked again. Over the years, however, a batsman gets as many decisions in his favour as against him. Much of the credit for this turn of events must go to the man who established the Code of Conduct, Colin Cowdrey.

Lord Cowdrey was the first chairman of the ICC who was not also president of the MCC and his appointment was the first major step in breaking away from the MCC. The world's oldest cricket club had run the ICC since 15 June 1909, when representatives of England, Australia and South Africa, the Foundation Members, met at Lord's and founded what was known as the Imperial Cricket Conference. They did an excellent job in spreading cricket all over the world. Membership was confined to the governing bodies of cricket within the British Commonwealth where Test cricket was played. The declared function of the ICC was 'to be responsible in co-operation with member countries for the development, co-ordination, regulation and promotion of the game of cricket worldwide'.

India, New Zealand and the West Indies were elected as Full Members in 1926, Pakistan in 1952, Sri Lanka in 1981 and Zimbabwe in 1992. South Africa ceased to be a member on leaving the British Commonwealth in 1961 but was elected a Full Member in 1991 under the new name of the United Cricket Board of South Africa.

In 1965 the member countries decided to end the link with the British Commonwealth and while the acronym remained the same, the name changed to the International Cricket Conference, meeting every midsummer at Lord's. This led to an expansion with newly admitted Associate Members entitled to one vote and the Full Members two. There are now twenty-three Associate Members, all countries where cricket is deemed to be firmly established and organized. In addition, there are thirteen Affiliate Members where cricket is played under the Laws of the game. They have no voting rights.

There was a further change in 1989 when new rules were adopted and the name was changed to the International Cricket Council. The motivating factor behind the change was the need to take the ICC away from merely being a forum for discussion in which only recommendations to Members could be made to a meeting in which decisions that are binding on Members are taken to ensure effective management of the game internationally.

Founder Members England and Australia had the right of veto and the West Indies felt that was wrong and needed changing. A working party was set up comprising George Mann of the MCC and the TCCB, Raman Subba Row of the TCCB and Joe Buzaglo of Gibraltar, representing the Associates. Their report in 1989 recommended a review of the veto. In 1992 the West Indies drafted a seven-page resolution that was presented to the ICC summer meeting and called for the veto to be abolished. It was an excellent piece of work and the Members, including England

and Australia, could not fault it. My great friend Judge Eric Bishop, a recently retired judge in Barbados and a former schoolfriend, drafted it for the West Indies Board. As we said in our resolution, 'it is an anachronism and its removal can only serve to enhance the intended spirit and working of the rules and the universal image of the ICC'. After a lengthy debate, our resolution was accepted unanimously the following year.

Another anachronism that was removed was the MCC's role in ICC affairs. That changed in 1993 when we voted in favour of no longer automatically having the MCC president appointing the chairman of the ICC, and also having a chief executive to run our affairs rather than the secretary of the MCC. David Richards, chief executive of the Australian Board, became our chief executive and has been doing a sound job ever since. The offices of the ICC have always been at Lord's and we saw no reason to change that, and David moved to the London area.

The West Indies Board has moved around the Caribbean and is now in Antigua, where the government made certain concessions to help with the move. Now that the Board has expanded it is unlikely it will move again.

In 1994, the ICC took a further step forward with the setting up of commercial operations. There is now a Development Committee under the chairmanship of Dr Ali Bacher. The ICC is run by an Executive Board which included one representative from each of the Test-playing countries, three from the Associates, the chairmen of the three subcommittees and the president and chief executive. Members of this Board have included Sir John Anderson (New Zealand), Khalid Mahmoud (Pakistan), P. Chingoka (Zimbabwe), Raj Singh Dungarpur (India), Raymond White (South Africa), Lord MacLaurin (England), D. Rangatunga (Sri Lanka), D. W. Rogers (Australia), P. H. O. Rousseau (West Indies), S. H. Chowdhury (Bangladesh), J. Rayani (Kenya) and HRH Tunku Imran (Malaysia). Regular contact is maintained and decisions can be made via tele-conferences, whereas in the past binding decisions could only be reached at the annual conference in London. I expect more frequent meetings will be held to enhance the decision-making process.

Each Full Member pays an annual subscription of fifteen thousand pounds, with Associate Members paying one thousand pounds. Profits from World Cups are split 75 per cent to the Full Members and 25 per cent to the Associates. The Cricket Committee has been able to standardize such matters as the number of overs in one-day matches at fifty, the quota of bouncers bowled in Tests to two instead of one, the criteria of stoppages for poor light, when a new ball can be taken in Tests (eighty overs), regulations concerning footmarks, the covering of pitches, the number of overs to be bowled each day in a Test (ninety) and a host of other matters.

The ICC had to ask referees to attend the tossing-up ceremony before the start of Tests because there have been two instances in the last year or two when there was a dispute between the two captains about who had won the toss. The referee now takes the coin to be used and shows it to the visiting captain to make sure he understands what is 'heads' and what is 'tails'. There is no problem in England, where the Queen's head is on one side of the coin and something very distinctive is on the other. In Barbados we have a flying fish on one side. In India and Pakistan they have something else. The regulations are strict about how many TV crews can be present during the filming of the toss. We do not want too many people crowding around.

One of the reasons why there is less chit-chat out in the middle is that at most Test matches there is now a stump microphone that picks up everything that is said. Ian Healy's voice exclaiming, 'Bowled Warney,' has been a recent feature of matches involving Australia, although I understand a lot of the keeper's comments are now edited out. There is a split-second delay between the time of the comment being made and its relay over the air, so the producer can make any necessary cuts.

We are investigating the possibility of beaming the unedited sound from the stump microphone into the referee's room so he can hear exactly what is being said, so if there is sledging he can act. The stump cameras and microphones can cost anything up to five thousand pounds, which is why the TV companies use special runners to race on to the field at the end of a match to ensure it is retrieved before a fan gets it. Once at Lord's a fan got there first and the stump camera was found the next day in a pub.

Throwing is another part of the game that has occupied the ICC over the years. Our policy is to try to save a player's career, not curtail it. If an umpire or referee reports that he has concerns about a bowler's action, we see that he is filmed. If a breach of the Law is being committed we can then speak to the player and see that he is coached to put the fault right. One or two players in the past few years have had their action examined in his way. No one has been banned and we do not intend to use that sanction unless it becomes absolutely necessary. Muttiah Muralitharan, the Sri Lankan spinner who bowled out England at the Oval in 1998, had his action looked at on video and the experts' opinion was that he had not infringed the Law.

The excessive use of bouncers was another problem, chiefly at the time of the West Indies' ascendancy when four fast bowlers operated in rotation. We have now changed the Law to allow two bouncers an over and that seems to satisfy everyone. The bouncer should be a surprise weapon; if it is used too much, it no longer ranks as a surprise. The umpire can still use that part of the Law concerning intimidation if he thinks a batsman is unable to defend himself when being exposed to short-pitched bowling. There is no change there. My personal view is that fewer bouncers are being bowled these days. They are a waste of energy against batsmen who move inside the line and let them go. Only when a batsman shows signs of not being able to cope does the bowler up the tempo. There are some bowlers who are bowling better now there is a limit of two an over. They are pitching the ball up more.

The ICC is currently investigating the best means of arriving at the target score in one-day matches. This is the score the side batting second needs to make to win when there has been a stoppage due to the weather. At the moment we are using the Duckworth–Lewis method invented by two cricket-mad Lancastrian mathematicians. It works better than previous methods tried because it takes into account wickets lost. I do not think it is the perfect solution: it is a complicated formula and the public needs to understand what is going on. We have a duty to avoid any confusion.

The vexed question of over rates has received a lot of attention. We have now standardized the daily total at ninety in six hours' play in Tests, a fair compromise in view of varying climatic conditions around the world. Any reasonably balanced bowling attack should be able to get through ninety overs in a day.

I do not believe the majority of spectators are unduly bothered about over rates, but there will be some people who are angered if they pay a lot of money to see a day's play and lose out on a number of overs. Pakistan and India have the worst records on over rates despite having more spin bowling than many other countries. In 1998–9 Pakistan were responsible for nine infringements of the fifteen-overs-an-hour requirement and India eight. Sri Lanka and England did not pay a single fine in that year. Countries often exceed the time allotted but the referee can make deductions for drinks intervals, injury and unscheduled interruptions.

One area where we may have been too zealous is the granting of wides. I often see a wide signalled in a one-day match when the ball has passed reasonably close to the batsman, especially on the offside. When it is down the leg I think that umpires *do* have to be strict with bowlers attempting to limit the batsmen's ability to score. However, there are still too many wides being called on both sides of the wicket and they can be the difference between winning and losing.

From the early days of cricket the players have always interfered with the ball. It used to be by raising the seam with fingernails to give spinners a better chance of turning the ball, or quicker bowlers the advantage of movement caused by the change in the aerodynamics of the ball. In later years a new type of ball tampering has emerged: the ball is scuffed on one side and polished on the other to help the bowler achieve what is called reverse swing. I must say I have never seen this practice used in a match in which I have been involved as a player, manager or administrator, but I know it was prevalent because the umpires have reported it and there has been plenty of talk about how to legislate against it. I am opposed to any form of interference with the ball and do not accept that on good batting pitches the bowler should be allowed to redress things by treating the ball in such a way that he gains an advantage. By all means shine the ball in the normal way; but to try anything else is cheating.

Ball tampering came to our notice at ICC in the early 1990s when it was claimed that Waqar Younis and Wasim Akram were swinging the old ball much more than the new one. Batsmen who had faced them and others were suspicious of their methods, but these two great bowlers insisted they were not breaking the law, merely letting one side of the ball deteriorate in the usual way while polishing the other side. For their defence it was said the shine disappeared so quickly that the bowler had to do something to enable him to stand a chance of dismissing batsmen. It must be emphasized that no bowler was penalized by the ICC for interference with the ball. The only person punished was the England captain Michael Atherton after the ICC referee Peter

Burge found him guilty of rubbing dirt into the side of the ball. He was fined two thousand pounds by the English Cricket Board and the ICC took no further action. Atherton claimed he had the dirt in his pocket to help keep his fingers dry on a hot day.

The ICC acted to prevent ball tampering becoming a problem by telling the umpires to have random checks on the state of the ball. Fielders are supposed to give the ball to the umpire at the end of an over if required. Since this measure was introduced there has not been a single complaint about ball tampering. These spot checks have also removed the possibility of players applying hair cream, lip salve or any other illegal substance to the ball. When I was playing the use of hair cream to aid the shining process was commonplace. Many of the leading bowlers wore what seemed to be an excessive amount of hair cream. It was cheating and it has now been eliminated, as has the use of bottle tops to rough up the surface of the ball.

During the Commonwealth Games cricketers were tested for drugs for the first time. The ICC has no drug-testing programme of its own and is unlikely to start one in the immediate future. Drug testing is an expensive business and we do not believe drugs are a problem in the sport. Ian Botham was banned in England after admitting he took a recreational drug, but that was an isolated case. If a problem did emerge, I am sure we would deal with it.

A substantial sponsorship from National Grid enabled the ICC to launch an important change, the introduction of independent umpires at Test level, one from abroad to serve with an umpire from the home country. We were reluctant to make both umpires independent because we realized that would restrict the progress of younger umpires in the home nation. We wanted to start this scheme to avoid any suspicion that some umpires were giving 'hometown' decisions, an accusation routinely made to us by captains and managers whose perception was that the officials were not as impartial as they ought to be. The 'hometown' umpires, if there were any, have now disappeared. There are still bad decisions being made but they are accepted with better grace if the umpire responsible comes from a neutral country.

Umpires are marked by the captains and the referees and we usually take little or no notice of an adverse report. The marks are totted up and we have a table at the ICC office that indicates the performance levels of the twenty umpires on the ICC panel. There were a number of questionable decisions in 1998 and we are now examining ways of seeing that those in the top half of the table are chosen for the key Tests. We want to avoid sending an inexperienced umpire to officiate in a series where the pressures on him are greatest. Appointments are made by David Richards, ICC cricket operations manager Clive Hitchcock and myself. There is no retirement age for umpires but they are expected to pass rigorous medicals each year. Those with eyesight or hearing defects are likely to be removed from the list.

Punishments for players include suspensions and fines of up to 75 per cent of a player's match fee. Australian wicketkeeper Ian Healy was suspended for two matches for showing dissent in Calcutta in 1997. Raman Subba Row made the decision, and he also suspended the Pakistan captain Aamir Sohail for one match for showing dissent in Melbourne. The players recognize and accept that there is no right of appeal. That is as it should be. If they were able to appeal it would drag out the process, one development we sought to avoid when we brought the scheme in seven years ago.

One of the ICC's main problems was the hosting of World Cups. Several countries wanted to organize them and there was criticism of the plan to allow England to stage the 1996 World Cup after staging the inaugural three tournaments, in 1975, 1979 and 1983. The meeting in 1995 which thrashed out a compromise to allow India, Pakistan and Sri Lanka jointly to take over the

1996 event was described by Alan Smith, one of England's representatives, as 'the most acrimonious meeting I have ever attended'. It went on until late at night at Lord's and I had to agree it was not a pleasant experience. The vote in favour of England was 5–4 but since a two-thirds majority was needed there was deadlock. Most of the Associate Members favoured the India, Pakistan and Sri Lanka bid which guaranteed £100,000 each for the Associates against the £65,000 guaranteed by England. Sir Colin Cowdrey, who presided, insisted that a decision should be made that night. Doug Insole, one of England's representatives, had to leave because his car was in a car park in east London that closed at midnight.

A solution was eventually found when England withdrew their bid on the provision that two conditions were met: first, that a chief executive of the ICC would be appointed by July and, second, that England would have the right to stage the 1999 World Cup. David Richards was duly appointed chief executive five months later. A further part of the deal was that South Africa would have the 2003 tournament. There had been a great deal of jockeying for position during the exhausting day before John Stephenson, who was then acting as ICC secretary, emerged at 11.30 p.m. to announce to the press that a settlement had been reached.

I have to say that when more than one country is involved in organizing a World Cup the relations between those countries improves. That happened in the 1987 tournament with India and Pakistan working well together and being understanding of each other's problems and also in Australia and New Zealand in 1991.

A major setback for the ICC was the refusal of the Australian and West Indies teams to play in Sri Lanka in the 1996 World Cup after it was felt it would be risky to play there. A bomb planted by the Tamil Tigers terrorist group had gone off in the centre of Colombo not long before and the Australian players said that no amount of security would be able to protect them if a similar bomb was detonated while they were playing their matches on the island. India and Pakistan flew their teams to Colombo to play an exhibition match to show solidarity with the Sri Lankans. The Australians and West Indians forfeited points as a result of their boycott. The West Indies team later lost by 73 runs to Kenya.

At a press conference in Calcutta before the tournament started it was suggested that Australia and the West Indies were indulging in a vendetta against the Third World. I had to point out that the West Indies were part of the Third World! The meeting preceding the press conference was the most difficult I had chaired at the ICC. Tempers flared and the strange thing about it was that, at the start, there were two teams that were refusing to play in Sri Lanka but by 6 p.m. there were four teams refusing to play in Sri Lanka! Eventually, better sense prevailed and the other two countries changed their minds. I was most disappointed at the press conference because the ICC was putting forward one point of view and Pilcom, the organizers of the tournament, were putting forward another. I feel the ICC has to consider running these events itself, rather than handing over responsibility to another organization, in this case Pilcom. FIFA, the world football body, runs the football World Cup itself with expert help. We should do the same. The good thing to emerge from the 1996 event was that Sri Lanka, international newcomers who played the most positive cricket throughout, came through to win in the final, beating Australia by seven wickets in Lahore. They introduced a new approach to the limited-overs game with their strategy of scoring as many runs as possible by taking risks in the first fifteen overs. This technique has since been adopted by many other countries. The Sri Lankan team's success had a hugely beneficial effect on cricket in their country.

The semi-final in Calcutta between Sri Lanka and the host

nation India was marred by shameful crowd scenes when it became obvious that the home side were not going to get anywhere near Sri Lanka's 251 for eight. Sections of the crowd of one hundred thousand at Eden Gardens turned their anger on Mohammed Azharuddin's side, setting fire to seating and throwing bottles on to the outfield. Clive Lloyd, the match referee, along with the umpires, took the teams off and the match was abandoned with Sri Lanka being awarded a place in the Wills World Cup final. It was ironic that the India and Pakistan Boards had gone to such lengths to win the right to host the tournament only for it to end so disappointingly for them. It was in stark contrast to the 1987 event in those countries, which passed off without incident and had proved such a success.

The ICC's decision to appoint development officers around the world to further the expansion of the game into the areas where resources are limited has been rightly hailed as a major success. In 1998 we appointed a development manager to push this plan ahead with the long-term objective being to make cricket a world sport, as opposed to the current situation in which the game is dominated by English-speaking countries. This will take many years to achieve. Cricket is not like football, which is a simpler, less costly game to play and organize.

A working party has also been set up to examine ways of introducing a world championship of Test cricket. We would all like such a championship to come about but the difficulties are immense. Fixtures between the major nations have been arranged for years to come and the working party has to decide whether these matches can be used in a championship or whether special dates should be set aside for shortened series, some taking place in England in the second half of the summer and the others elsewhere during the English winter. My personal view is that it will be some years before there is a world championship for five-day cricket, much as I would like to see one.

Another complication is that there is pressure for the World Cup to be staged every two years instead of every four. I am resolutely against that. If the World Cup was held more frequently it would lose its appeal. Four years is right to maintain interest.

21   *Strike!*

When the West Indian players went on strike in November 1998 and refused to go to South Africa for the inaugural series it was suggested that this was a first in the history of West Indian cricket. This is not so. In my time as a West Indies administrator there were at least two occasions when the players wanted more money and were becoming militant. Each time we were able to sort it out behind closed doors. The West Indian cricketer always wants more money; to do so is a fact of cricketing life. We were the same in my day, although I have to say we had more reason to be unhappy at our reward. Most of us were considered amateurs and played only for expenses.

Former West Indies Board president, Peter Short, suggested at the time of the 1998 dispute that I should act as a mediator because of my experience in this field as a result of my employment outside cricket. This was very generous of him, but in my opinion it was a dispute that had to be settled by the West Indies Board, the president and the West Indies Players' Association. Ali Bacher, managing director of the United Cricket Board of South Africa, called me on a number of occasions with updates of what was happening but I did not have all the facts. What I did know was that during the Wills Tournament in Bangladesh, which I attended, the contract row between the two sides had not been resolved and the players had not signed their contracts for the tour of South Africa. There was a grave danger that the tour might not take place. Matters should not have been allowed to reach that stage.

The next thing I knew was that Brian Lara, the captain, and his vice-captain Carl Hooper were returning to London on the same flight as me after the Bangladesh tournament ended when they should have been flying to Johannesburg with the rest of the party. I did not think it was any of my business to find out why they had been rerouted the long way round. And at the time I did not know that they were intending to rendezvous with the players from the Caribbean who were coming in to London before going on to Johannesburg.

It was also a surprise to me to learn that the seven players who went with manager Clive Lloyd to South Africa were joining them at an expensive hotel near Heathrow to present a united front. Courtney Walsh, in his capacity as president of the Players' Association accepted a letter from Nelson Mandela given to him by Dr Bacher in front of a mass of TV cameras in the hotel lobby. This tour meant so much to South Africa as a nation and a people that the President himself had become involved.

The Board had met in Antigua and announced that their unanimous decision was to relieve Lara and Hooper of their positions. This was received with approval in some parts of the Caribbean but, as I expected, the majority were on the side of the players. In any cricket dispute in the West Indies the public is nearly always on the side of the players.

What surprised me about this episode was that David Holford, the chief executive of the West Indies Players' Association, flew to London early on but did not take part in the negotiations. And I was even more surprised that the Board's chief executive, Steve Camacho, was not included in the Board's delegation. I had honestly felt that when the Players' Association established an office in Barbados with a paid staff and financing assistance from the Bajan government and the West Indies Board they would have alleviated the communication problems that had existed in the past.

Joel Garner flew to London to represent the Board and discovered that the players, an agent and two lawyers advising them would only deal with the top man, Pat Rousseau. When he was a player Joel was always critical of administration but now he was on the other side, as an administrator, he could see the problems for himself.

There is more money coming into West Indies cricket, with commercial men running it, and it should be no surprise that the players want their share. There was a handsome sponsorship from Cable and Wireless, and money from a television company. I have always been wary of backing any pay demands from players because our game cannot be compared to English cricket, and more especially to cricket in Australia where peak attendances can sometimes total fifty thousand or more. Our players cannot really be expected to be paid as much as their English and Australian counterparts. Could the Prime Minister of Barbados expect to earn the same salary as the Prime Minister of Britain? I do not think so. There has to be compromise and good sense on both sides and there was a lack of both in the 1998 row.

Incidentally, I think Brian Lara has to come to terms with the success he has had. He is very knowledgeable about cricket and has shown himself to be an imaginative captain. Now he is in a position of power there are certain things he just cannot do. As a player Lara is one of the greatest the West Indies has produced. His record confirms that opinion, but if I had to choose between him and Sir Garfield Sobers for my left-hander in a world eleven I would definitely go for Sobers. Gary was a better batsman, even before you take into account his varied bowling. Lara has periods when he finds it difficult to maintain his standards and he needs to slow down a little and sort things out before he continues playing his extravagant and exciting shots. He did that in his innings of 213 in Jamaica in March 1999, thankfully, and again in his remarkable match-winning innings of 153 not out in Barbados. He has learned to curb his natural instincts until his form and confidence return. People always said the same about Viv Richards and he found it equally hard to restrain himself.

Lara showed against England in the 1998 series that he is prepared to gamble. He captained in the way the West Indian fans want their skippers to captain. But he is handicapped in that he does not have an outstanding side under him. It does not compare with the teams of the recent past and we need a number of younger players to emerge. Unfortunately, there is little sign of that happening.

Carl Hooper's record is now tarnished and he needs to rebuild his career in a positive way so that he can at last fulfil the talent he has always possessed. He is a very withdrawn person, and though he may give the appearance of not knowing the difference between right and wrong, I believe he can be managed. He is knowledgeable about the game as he showed in his brief time as captain of Guyana. As a batsman he has more time than most of his rivals to play his shots but he lets himself down because of his shot selection, hitting the ball in the air far more than a good player should, especially in Test cricket. If you keep hitting the ball in the air it is never long before you are caught. I do not rate his bowling too highly. He is quite an ordinary offspinner but the West Indies do not have too many in that department. In the past he bowled more than he should because there was no one else.

Courtney Walsh did not come out of the strike business too badly. As president of the Players' Association he had to front it up. He still retains his high standing in the game, a man who has always given his maximum. His bowling has improved as he has matured as a cricketer and so has his catching. In his role as president of the Players' Association he has had to take a lead and that may not have been his preference. He is a team man who always went along with the majority verdict. I doubt whether he would have initiated the stand-off between the Board and the players.

One of the points the players insisted on was that there should be extra security on the tour. They were worried that after the alleged mugging of two Pakistani players during the Pakistani tour they might be exposed to similar violence. The West Indies Board demanded guarantees of safety and Dr Bacher promised there would be twenty-four-hour protection of the team. It was ironic that the first person to be mugged was Pat Rousseau, the president of the Board, along with the respected Jamaican journalist Tony Becca. The two men were held up in Soweto and their watches and valuables stolen. 'It was frightening at the time but within a couple of minutes Tony was making jokes,' said Rousseau. The next day President Mandela arrived in person to apologize.

The timing could not have been worse for the South African government. The same day FIFA's general secretary Sepp Blatter arrived to present an award to President Mandela and discuss the possibility of the 2006 World Cup being held in the country. If security cannot be guaranteed, South Africa's chances of being chosen to host the tournament, ahead of England and Germany, the other two countries in the bidding, would diminish considerably. Sadly, Johannesburg has the reputation of being one of the world's most violent cities.

It remains to be seen whether the agreement worked out at the Radisson Edwardian Hotel in London in November can lead to a lasting peace in West Indian cricket. The players wanted assurances about pay and conditions for future tours and many promises were made. What West Indies cricket now needs is a period of stability.

Lara's side on that 1998-9 tour was completely outplayed in every department of the game. All the weaknesses of our cricket were exposed. The South African public were looking forward to seeing the exciting cricket they had read about over the years and were let down. It was the first whitewash – a 5–0 series defeat – that the West Indies had experienced. Unfortunately, Lara didn't score a century in the series, and hadn't scored one in the previous thirteen Tests. Much work now has to be done at all levels to restore our standing in the game. In the past, West Indies cricket has been successful as a result of the natural talent of its players. Today, the West Indies need to concentrate on using technology – including videos for coaching purposes – at every level in order to improve our game.

One striking observation I made on the tour was that the West Indies are the only team playing international cricket today where not one player dives to save runs in the field. I was told that a specialist coach had been hired to train players in this skill, but that our players had been in London at the time, negotiating with the Board for increased fees!

This controversy, at such a late stage, was damaging to team spirit and morale, and things got worse rather than better. The lack of talent and commitment played a major role in the defeats. I watched three of the Tests and became increasingly disillusioned. Our team had great difficulty batting for a whole day, and our back-up bowlers could not match the professionalism of their South African counterparts.

Lara's magnificent innings in the second and third Tests against the Australians brought a dramatic change in his own fortunes and those of the team, but it is only a beginning. He is almost a born-again cricketer and I can see him getting even better.

22　The Future

It concerns me that, because of the lifestyles of the members of the modern generation, fewer people will be able to watch Test matches played during the day. People seem to be working longer and harder, and the danger is that only those who are retired or on holiday will be free to attend Tests.

In some countries this is not such a problem. When there are attractive opponents the attendances in the West Indies, England and Australia are generally good. In India and Pakistan the demand is for one-day cricket and those matches are usually watched by full-house crowds. In New Zealand attendances at Tests are not good. In South Africa the United Cricket Board is doing a tremendous amount to promote Test cricket but I noticed in the last series against the West Indies that there were still many empty seats at the Wanderers ground.

Crowds are the lifeblood of any sport and they inspire players to greater achievements. To play in front of empty stands reduces sport as a spectacle and we have to see that this does not happen as we enter the next century.

West Indian crowds have always been known for their wit and humour. One of the best comments I heard was at a home Test when J. K. Holt was batting particularly slowly. At the time a Jamaican Test cricketer, Leslie Hylton, was languishing in jail awaiting execution after being found guilty of murder. Someone in the crowd shouted out, 'Save Hylton, hang Holt!'

Calypsos have always been a feature of our cricket and when Ian Botham was captain on a tour of the Caribbean he came out to bat when his side was not doing well to a chorus of 'Captain, captain the ship is sinking', which was one of the popular calypsos of the time sung by the Trinidadian Gypsy.

West Indian crowds are very knowledgeable about the finer points of the game. They are unlikely to applaud if a batsman snicks the ball for four. This appreciation of the proper skills is traditional. It comes from their upbringing. Most West Indians love the game and understand it.

Crowds in India and Pakistan may be just as noisy but spectators there understand less about the game. Their crowds tend to be excitable and it is not unusual to see missiles thrown on to the outfield when something displeases them.

Players like plenty of noise and encouragement. What they dread is the absence of any atmosphere. Australian crowds are pretty noisy and generally good-humoured, although there have been drink problems, especially at day–night matches, which have concerned the authorities.

English crowds can be on the quiet side. Lord's is an example, but if a player shows some skill there he is always generously applauded.

I do not approve of the Mexican Wave. It has nothing to do with cricket and is tiresome. Some countries have introduced music at matches to liven things up and I have no objection to that, as long as it is not in the form of beating drums or some other percussion instrument which is played incessantly without any tune to the annoyance of other spectators. In Trinidad the Trini Possee starts up between overs and the general view is that it adds to the enjoyment.

There has been a debate in England about admitting spectators in fancy dress. Lancashire, for example, said they would ban anyone wearing outlandish costumes or outfits that affected the view of others. Personally, I do not think cricket is the place for fancy dress.

The West Indies have always had 'characters' at matches who amuse the audience. In Barbados the late King Dyal ruled at Kensington Oval for a long time. He turned up most days in different-coloured suits, carrying an umbrella, and he always supported England when they played at the ground. I think he felt he had a kinship with the monarchy and thought he had to support Her Majesty's men.

If the slow decline in attendances at Tests in some countries is not reversed I foresee the time when they will become day–night encounters. Day–night Tests would enable people to attend after work and could attract a new audience of younger men and women. Football took off in England when floodlit competitions were introduced and watching a game under lights makes it faster and somehow more enjoyable. There are lots of difficulties to be overcome, not least the cost. It is very expensive to install floodlights and maintenance costs are also high. The grounds need to be dual purpose, with other sports being played outside the cricket season. Cricket can no longer afford to have its stadiums lying idle for most of the year.

Not being able to meet expenses through match receipts has always been a problem in cricket. Sponsors have helped to make up the shortfall, and now that television has entered the sport in a big way money from that source is proving invaluable. We must not let television take over, however, by dictating starting times and rescheduling matches to suit their programming. As American sport has shown, the more the big matches are shown live, the greater the interest in the sport. TV acts as a promotional boost for sport and we have to harness its advantages.

It is absolutely paramount that Test cricket survives. It is the highest form of the sport, played at its best by the top players without any restrictions being placed on them. If you ask those most closely associated with Test cricket, the players, the umpires and the administrators, if they want it to continue they are unanimous in saying that they do, even the youngest of the players. One-day cricket has its place, bringing excitement and glamour, and has the advantage of being over in a day. But it should never replace Tests. We do not remember who won a certain one-day competition held five years ago because there are so many one-day matches. But we remember what has happened in Test matches: who won, who set the records and who won the plaudits.

I am less concerned about the numbers of young players coming into the game. Most countries have development programmes and more coaches are teaching more youngsters. Maybe fewer youngsters with natural talent are coming through because of the lives they lead. Everything has to be done in a hurry and children have less time to play what is essentially a slow game. The less time they have to play, the more important is the role of the coach in helping them take short cuts and encouraging them to fulfil the talent they possess.

In such countries as India, Pakistan and Sri Lanka I have seen children playing cricket in the streets, the parks, the backyards and the spare pieces of land. These three countries have no worries about where the talent is coming from. The United Cricket Board in South Africa is trying to encourage the same response from young blacks but that will be a slow process. In South Africa the non-whites are passionate about football, and cricket comes a long way behind.

The policy of the ICC is to encourage the spread of cricket to as many countries as possible. The total of twenty-three Associated Members is expected to rise quickly. We must encourage the indigenous populations in those countries to take up the game. Where it is being run and played by expatriates from traditional cricket-playing countries it will not put down the same roots.

There has been a levelling out of standards among the nine Test-playing countries. One country is no longer dominant as the West Indies were in the 1970s and 1980s. The countries are beating each other now and it was satisfying for those of us who campaigned for the admission of Zimbabwe as a Full Member of the ICC to see them win their first victory away from home in Pakistan in December 1998. In Zimbabwe they do not have many clubs or many players, yet their cricket has advanced at an amazing pace. The Sri Lankans have made great progress since their admission, and that looks set to continue.

The West Indies were represented by its constituent countries in the Commonwealth Games in 1998 and that led to the thought that Barbados, Jamaica, Antigua, Trinidad and the various Leeward and Windward islands should become separate entities and be admitted to memberhip of the ICC as individual Full Members. I do not favour that at all as it would not work. Most of the islands are not strong or populous enough to support themselves. We need to stick together to preserve cricket in the West Indies. The West Indian governments are talking about confederation, and for cricket administrators to initiate a split would be a retrograde step.

The decline of cricket in England in terms of Test results cannot be good for the game overall. England gave this great game to the world and needs to continue to play a leading part. I cannot see their plight being relieved until they get cricket back into the schools. In Barbados there is now greater concentration on academic performance in our schools, but cricket is still played in school time and two schools sides take part in the senior competition of the Barbados Cricket Association: Combined Schools North and Combined Schools South. The boys playing for these sides compete against the best senior players on the island and it is good experience for them. The former West Indian and English county professional and coach Franklyn Stephenson plays for one of the sides in the island competition in his forties. And he is still bowling that tantalizing slow ball!

In England I understand very little cricket is played in state schools and cricket fields are disappearing rapidly. Only the public schools continue to play the game and many of the better players they produce are lost to cricket when they go into well-paid jobs in preference to trying their luck in the hard grind of the county circuit.

The 2003 World Cup is scheduled for South Africa, and I am sure it will be a success. They have the grounds, the transportation and the communications. The only major worry is security. The next World Cup after that is booked for the West Indies and work is already under way on improving the capacities and comfort of grounds and building new media centres. It will be a tremendous boost to the region to hold the first event of this kind in the Caribbean and our cricket will benefit from it enormously.

One-day cricket is here to stay and there will doubtless be changes to improve it and make it more exciting to watch. I cannot agree with turning it into a shorter form of instant cricket in an attempt to reach a much younger audience. They have tried this in New Zealand with Cricket Max, the brainchild of that country's former Test captain Martin Crowe, and it has also been played in Australia. I see no need for it in the West Indies.

Women's cricket continues to develop around the world with a World Cup similar to the men's version and the various Boards helping its advancement. In New Zealand the women's association has a representative on the full New Zealand Board. Unfortunately, women's cricket does not attract crowds. It is a long way from being self-supporting and the men must help it all they can.

I see a bright future for cricket. The game that took me around the world is expanding and capturing the imagination of millions of youngsters in many countries. We must see that they have every chance to fulfil their dreams.

·

APPENDICES

Career Record

Date of Birth – 17 January 1926.

HONOURS

1966 – O.B.E. Most Excellent Order of the British Empire.
Contribution to Cricket in Barbados, Guyana and West Indies.

1970 – A.A. Golden Arrow of Achievement Award.
Contribution to Cricket in Guyana.

1991 – G.C.M. Gold Crown of Merit.
Contribution to Cricket and Cricket Administration in the Caribbean.

1993 – K.A. Knighthood.
Contribution to Cricket and Cricket Administration in the West Indies and Internationally.

ORGANIZATIONS

President Guyana Cricket Board of Control – 1968–70.
Senior Vice-President Barbados Cricket Association – 1972–87.
President West Indies Cricket Board of Control – 1988–93.
Chairman International Cricket Council – 1993–present.

Managed West Indies Cricket teams:

1969	*To England.*
1973–4	*Australia in West Indies.*
1975	*1st World Cup in England.*
1976	*To England.*
1979	*2nd World Cup in England.*
1980	*To England.*
1987	*3rd World Cup in India and Pakistan.*

CRICKETING CAREER
(Outstanding Achievements)

Represented Barbados from age sixteen – 1942–54.
Represented Guyana – 1954–63 – when employed as Cricket Organizer and Coach.
Represented West Indies – 1948–60.
Test match batting – 44 Tests, 74 innings, not out 7. Total runs – 3798. Highest score – 220. Centuries – 15. Average – 56.68.
Scored a century in each innings of a Test match on two occasions during one tour – against Australia, 1955.
168 not out at Lords, 1950, when West Indies won its first Test match in England.
First-class cricket – highest score – 314 not out for Barbados v. Trinidad, 1946.

FOOTBALL

Represented Barbados in 1940s.

APPENDIX 2 *Statistical Record*

Information supplied by
The Association of Cricket Statisticians and Historians

FIRST-CLASS RECORD (BATTING AND FIELDING)

Year		M	I	NO	Runs	HS	Ave	100	50	ct	st
1941–2		1	2	0	8	8	4.00	-	-	-	-
1942		2	3	0	187	70	62.33	-	3	1	-
1942–3		2	4	0	148	58	37.00	-	2	-	-
1943–4		2	3	0	100	55	33.33	-	1	-	1
1944–5		4	7	0	348	125	49.71	2	1	4	1
1945–6		2	4	1	397	314*	132.33	1	-	5	2
1946–7		2	4	0	88	42	22.00	-	-	1	-
1947–8		6	10	2	275	120	34.37	1	-	14	5
1948–9	India, Pakistan, Ceylon	15	22	4	1366	152	75.88	5	7	24	3
1949–50		2	3	1	293	211*	146.50	1	1	3	-
1950	England	25	36	6	1674	168*	55.80	7	5	30	18
1950–1		2	4	0	409	209	102.25	1	2	1	-
1951–2	Australia, New Zealand	13	23	1	1098	186	49.90	4	6	12	3
1952–3		6	8	1	508	125	72.57	2	2	9	-
1953	England	2	4	0	141	115	35.25	1	-	4	-
1953–4		6	12	2	723	220	72.30	3	3	4	-
1954	England	1	2	1	42	39*	42.00	-	-	-	-
1954–5		7	13	0	962	155	74.00	5	4	5	-
1955–6		3	4	0	149	130	37.25	1	-	2	-
1956–7		2	2	0	90	64	45.00	-	1	4	-
1957	England	21	36	5	1414	131	45.61	3	7	28	-
1957–8		5	6	1	414	145	82.80	1	2	4	-
1958–9		2	4	1	195	70	65.00	-	2	2	-
1959–60		4	6	1	277	83	55.40	-	3	5	-
1960–1		1	2	1	154	108	154.00	1	-	-	-
1961–2		3	5	1	90	60	22.50	-	1	6	-
1962–3		1	2	0	17	13	8.50	-	-	3	-
1963–4		4	7	0	271	105	38.71	1	1	3	-
Total		**146**	**238**	**29**	**11838**	**314***	**56.64**	**40**	**54**	**174**	**33**

*Not out

FIRST-CLASS RECORD (BOWLING)

Year		O	M	R	W	Ave	Best	5wi
1942		5	0	20	0	-	-	-
1942–3		4	0	24	1	24.00	1/24	-
1943–4		4.7	0	12	1	12.00	1/1	-
1946–7		6	2	7	0	-	-	-
1947–8		3	2	2	0	-	-	-
1948–9	India, Pakistan, Ceylon	63	18	130	1	130.00	1/26	-
1949–50		50.3	11	124	8	15.50	4/26	-
1950	England	12	6	22	0	-	-	-
1950–1		13	5	29	0	-	-	-
1951–2	Australia, New Zealand	8	3	8	1	8.00	1/8	-
1952–3		61	26	88	2	44.00	2/12	-
1953	England	4	0	13	0	-	-	-
1953–4		83.3	38	159	8	19.87	4/42	-
1954–5		72	24	156	4	39.00	3/50	-
1955–6		50	14	116	3	38.66	1/15	-
1956–7		4	2	2	0	-	-	-
1957	England	8	2	28	0	-	-	-
1957–8		23	10	29	0	-	-	-
1958–9		19.3	2	68	0	-	-	-
1959–60		38	8	114	1	114.00	1/43	-
1961–2		7	3	12	0	-	-	-
1963–4		35.1	8	106	5	21.20	5/41	1
Total		**574.5**	**184**	**1269**	**35**	**36.25**	**5/41**	**1**

TEST RECORD (BATTING AND FIELDING)

Season	Opponent	M	I	NO	Runs	HS	Ave	100	50	ct	st
1947–8	England	4	7	1	133	45	22.16	0	0	11	5
1948–9	India	5	7	0	452	152	64.57	2	2	9	2
1950	England	4	6	1	229	168*	45.80	1	0	4	3
1951–2	Australia	3	6	0	87	60	14.50	0	1	4	1
1951–2	New Zealand	2	3	0	199	115	66.33	1	1	2	-
1952–3	India	5	7	1	457	125	76.16	2	1	7	-
1953–4	England	5	10	2	698	220	87.25	3	3	3	-
1954–5	Australia	5	10	0	827	155	82.70	5	2	5	-
1957	England	5	10	1	247	90	27.44	0	1	3	-
1957–8	Pakistan	4	5	1	385	145	96.25	1	2	3	-
1959–60	England	2	3	0	84	53	28.00	0	1	2	-
Total		**44**	**74**	**7**	**3798**	**220**	**56.68**	**15**	**14**	**53**	**11**

TEST RECORD (BOWLING)

Season	Opponent	O	M	R	W	Ave	Best	5wi
1948–9	India	3	0	12	0	-	-	-
1950	England	4	1	12	0	-	-	-
1952–3	India	35	14	48	2	24.00	2/12	-
1953–4	England	53	24	94	4	23.50	3/52	-
1954–5	Australia	71	24	152	4	38.00	3/50	-
1957	England	1	0	4	0	-	-	-
1957–8	Pakistan	12	5	16	0	-	-	-
1959–60	England	20	4	70	1	70.00	1/43	-
Total		**199**	**72**	**408**	**11**	**37.09**	**3/50**	-

RECORD OF EACH VENUE (BATTING AND FIELDING)

WEST INDIES	M	I	NO	Runs	HS	Ave	100	50	ct	st
Bridgetown	23	39	3	2169	220	60.25	5	13	23	1
Georgetown	19	27	3	1227	145	51.12	4	6	27	2
Port-of-Spain	15	27	2	1437	314*	57.48	5	6	19	3
Kingston	11	20	2	1257	155	69.83	6	4	8	3
Berbice	1	2	1	13	8	13.00	-	-	-	-
Total	**69**	**115**	**11**	**6103**	**314***	**58.68**	**20**	**29**	**77**	**9**

ENGLAND	M	I	NO	Runs	HS	Ave	100	50	ct	st
Lord's	6	12	1	452	168*	41.09	2	-	9	7
Kennington Oval	5	7	2	424	149	84.80	2	1	1	-
Edgbaston	3	5	0	195	90	39.00	-	1	2	-
Old Trafford	3	5	2	127	63	42.33	-	1	3	-
Trent Bridge	3	4	0	147	115	36.75	1	-	2	1
Canterbury	2	4	1	213	131	71.00	1	-	4	-
Chesterfield	2	4	1	140	87	46.66	-	1	3	-
Hastings	2	3	1	145	103	72.50	1	-	3	1
Hove	2	2	1	87	67	87.00	-	1	6	3
Oxford (Christ Church)	2	2	0	78	58	39.00	-	1	2	1
Scarborough	2	4	1	145	121*	48.33	1	-	3	1
Southampton	2	3	0	96	58	32.00	-	1	-	-
Taunton	2	4	1	218	117*	72.66	1	1	-	-
Worcester	2	2	1	79	46*	79.00	-	-	4	-
Bradford	1	2	0	68	58	34.00	-	1	1	2
Bramall Lane	1	2	0	127	91	63.50	-	1	2	1
Cardiff	1	1	0	20	20	20.00	-	-	3	-
Cheltenham	1	1	0	126	126	126.00	1	-	-	-
Fenner's	1	1	0	86	86	86.00	-	1	3	-
Headingley	1	2	0	73	38	36.50	-	-	1	-
Ilford	1	2	0	79	50	39.50	-	1	3	-
Kingston-on-Thames	1	2	0	23	22	11.50	-	-	2	-
Leicester	1	-	-	-	-	-	-	-	3	-
Romford	1	2	0	118	115	59.00	1	-	2	-
Southend-on-Sea	1	2	0	5	5	2.50	-	-	-	1
Total	**49**	**78**	**12**	**3271**	**168***	**49.56**	**11**	**12**	**62**	**18**

INDIA	M	I	NO	Runs	HS	Ave	100	50	ct	st
Bombay	3	4	0	140	68	35.00	-	1	5	1
Calcutta	2	4	1	280	108	93.33	1	2	1	-
Allahabad	1	2	0	61	43	30.50	-	-	-	-
Baroda	1	2	1	144	73*	144.00	-	2	1	-
Jamshedpur	1	1	0	128	128	128.00	1	-	1	-
Madras	1	1	0	43	43	43.00	-	-	3	-
New Delhi	1	1	0	152	152	152.00	1	-	2	1
Patiala	1	1	0	75	75	75.00	-	1	4	-
Poona	1	2	0	121	120	60.50	1	-	-	1
Total	**12**	**18**	**2**	**1144**	**152**	**71.50**	**4**	**6**	**17**	**3**

AUSTRALIA	M	I	NO	Runs	HS	Ave	100	50	ct	st
Sydney	3	6	0	177	60	29.50	-	2	5	1
Brisbane	2	4	0	16	9	4.00	-	-	1	-
Melbourne	2	4	1	223	105	74.33	1	1	-	-
Adelaide	1	2	0	88	84	44.00	-	1	1	2
Hobart	1	1	0	186	186	186.00	1	-	-	-
Perth	1	2	0	61	50	30.50	-	1	2	-
Total	**10**	**19**	**1**	**751**	**186**	**41.72**	**2**	**5**	**10**	**3**

NEW ZEALAND	M	I	NO	Runs	HS	Ave	100	50	ct	st
Auckland	1	1	0	115	115	115.00	1	-	2	-
Christchurch	1	2	0	84	65	42.00	-	1	-	-
Wellington	1	1	0	148	148	148.00	1	-	-	-
Total	**3**	**4**	**0**	**347**	**148**	**86.75**	**2**	**1**	**2**	**-**

PAKISTAN	M	I	NO	Runs	HS	Ave	100	50	ct	st
Lahore	1	2	1	43	41	43.00	-	-	-	-

CEYLON	M	I	NO	Runs	HS	Ave	100	50	ct	st
Colombo	2	2	1	179	125*	179.00	1	1	7	-

| GRAND TOTAL | 146 | 238 | 29 | 11838 | 314* | 56.64 | 40 | 54 | 174 | 33 |

RECORD OF EACH VENUE (BOWLING)

WEST INDIES	O	M	R	W	Ave	Best	5wi
Bridgetown	224.4	73	517	15	34.46	4/26	-
Port-of-Spain	109	41	209	8	26.12	5/52	-
Kingston	82.1	25	192	9	21.33	5/41	1
Georgetown	58	13	142	1	142.00	1/43	-
Berbice	6	3	8	0	-	-	-
Total	**479.5**	**155**	**1068**	**33**	**32.36**	**5/41**	**1**

INDIA	O	M	R	W
Bombay	9	1	37	0
Calcutta	9	3	18	0
Jamshedpur	7	3	25	0
Total	**25**	**7**	**80**	**0**

ENGLAND	O	M	R	W
Kennington Oval	8	5	10	0
Canterbury	4	1	11	0
Old Trafford	4	1	12	0
Romford	4	0	13	0
Fenner's	3	1	13	0
Trent Bridge	1	0	4	0
Total	**24**	**8**	**63**	**0**

NEW ZEALAND	O	M	R	W	Ave	Best	5wi
Wellington	8	3	8	1	8.00	1/8	-

PAKISTAN	O	M	R	W
Lahore	18	9	24	0

CEYLON	O	M	R	W	Ave	Best	5wi
Colombo	20	2	26	1	26.00	1/26	-

GRAND TOTAL	O	M	R	W	Ave	Best	5wi
GRAND TOTAL	**574.5**	**184**	**1269**	**35**	**36.25**	**5/41**	**1**

FIRST-CLASS CENTURIES

1.	October 1944	125	Barbados v British Guiana	Bourda
2.	February 1945	103	Barbados v Trinidad	Queen's Park Oval
3.	February 1946	314*	Barbados v Trinidad	Queen's Park Oval
4.	January 1948	120	Barbados v M.C.C.	Kensington Oval
5.	November 1948	152	WEST INDIES v INDIA	New Delhi
6.	November 1948	129	West Indians v West Zone	Poona
7.	December 1948	108	WEST INDIES v INDIA	Calcutta
8.	January 1949	120	West Indians v Governor of Bihar's XI	Jamshedpur
9.	February 1949	125	West Indians v Ceylon	Colombo
10.	February 1950	211*	Barbados v British Guiana	Kensington Oval
11.	May 1950	128	West Indians v Surrey	Kennington Oval
12.	May 1950	117	West Indians v Somerset	Taunton
13.	June 1950	168*	WEST INDIES v ENGLAND	Lord's
14.	July 1950	149	West Indians v Surrey	Kennington Oval
15.	August 1950	126	West Indians v Gloucestershire	Cheltenham
16.	September 1950	103	West Indians v South of England	Hastings
17.	September 1950	121	West Indians v	
			Mr. H.D.G. Leveson-Gower's XI	Scarborough
18.	March 1951	209	Barbados v Trinidad	Kensington Oval
19.	January 1952	186	West Indians v Tasmania	Hobart
20.	January 1952	105	West Indians v Victoria	Melbourne
21.	February 1952	115	West Indians v New Zealand	Auckland
22.	February 1952	148	West Indians v Wellington	Wellington
23.	March 1953	125	WEST INDIES v INDIA	Bourda
24.	April 1953	118	WEST INDIES v INDIA	Sabina Park
25.	June 1953	115	Commonwealth XI v Essex	Romford
26.	February 1954	220	WEST INDIES v ENGLAND	Kensington Oval
27.	March 1954	124	WEST INDIES v ENGLAND	Queen's Park Oval
28.	March 1954	116	WEST INDIES v ENGLAND	Sabina Park
29.	March 1955	108	WEST INDIES v AUSTRALIA	Sabina Park
30.	April 1955	126	WEST INDIES v AUSTRALIA	Queen's Park Oval
31.	April 1955	110	WEST INDIES v AUSTRALIA	Queen's Park Oval
32.	June 1955	155	WEST INDIES v AUSTRALIA	Sabina Park
33.	June 1955	110	WEST INDIES v AUSTRALIA	Sabina Park
34.	March 1956	130	Barbados v E.W. Swanton's XI	Kensington Oval
35.	May 1957	117	West Indians v M.C.C.	Lord's
36.	May 1957	115	West Indians v Nottinghamshire	Trent Bridge
37.	August 1957	131	West Indians v Kent	Canterbury
38.	March 1958	145	WEST INDIES v PAKISTAN	Bourda
39.	April 1961	108	British Guiana v E.W. Swanton's XI	Bourda
40.	September 1963	105	F.M.M. Worrell's XI v C.C. Hunte's XI	Sabina Park

MODES OF DISMISSAL

First-Class	Ct	B	Lbw	RO	St	HWkt	NO	Total
	115	46	24	8	14	2	29	238

BATTING AND FIELDING RECORD AGAINST EACH TEST COUNTRY

Opponent	M	I	NO	Runs	HS	Ave	100	50	ct	st
England	20	36	5	1391	220	44.87	4	5	24	8
India	10	14	1	909	152	69.92	4	3	15	2
Australia	8	16	0	914	155	57.12	5	3	9	1
Pakistan	4	5	1	385	145	96.25	1	2	3	-
New Zealand	2	3	0	199	115	66.33	1	1	2	-
Total	**44**	**74**	**7**	**3798**	**220**	**56.68**	**15**	**14**	**53**	**11**

HUNDRED PARTNERSHIPS IN TESTS

SECOND WICKET
269   (145)   with G.St.A. Sobers (125)   v Pakistan   Georgetown   1957–8

THIRD WICKET
242   (126)   with E.D. Weeks (139)   v Australia   Port-of-Spain   1954–5
         (record for West Indies v Australia until Richardson & Richards 308 in 1983–84)
127   (110)   with E.D. Weeks (87*)   v Australia   Port-of-Spain   1954–5

FOURTH WICKET

267	(152)	with G.E. Gomez (101)	v India	New Delhi	1948–9
		(record for West Indies v India)			
213	(118)	with F.M.M. Worrell (237)	v India	Kingston	1952–3
		(record for West Indies v India in West Indies)			
188*	(88*)	with G.St.A. Sobers (365*)	v Pakistan	Kingston	1957–8
		(record for West Indies v Pakistan)			
179	(110)	with G.St.A. Sobers (64)	v Australia	Kingston	1954–5
		(record for West Indies v Australia until Lloyd & Kanhai 187 in 1972–3)			
165	(220)	with B.H. Pairaudeau (71)	v England	Bridgetown	1953–4
		(record for West Indies v England in West Indies until Sobers & Worrell 399 in 1959–60)			
130	(125)	with E.D. Weekes (86)	v India	Georgetown	1952–3
129	(65)	with F.M.M. Worrell (71)	v New Zealand	Christchurch	1951–2
		(record for West Indies v New Zealand until Weekes & Smith 162 in 1955–6)			
125	(73)	with F.M.M. Worrell (56)	v Australia	Georgetown	1954–5
110	(155)	with F.M.M. Worrell (61)	v Australia	Kingston	1954–5
101	(47)	with E.D. Weekes (207)	v India	Port-of-Spain	1952–3

FIFTH WICKET

189	(115)	with F.M.M. Worrell (100)	v New Zealand	Auckland	1951–2
		(record for West Indies v New Zealand)			
101*	(51*)	with D.St.E. Atkinson (53*)	v England	Port-of Spain	1953–4

SIXTH WICKET

211	(168*)	with G.E. Gomez (70)	v England	Lord's	1950
		(record for West Indies v England until Sobers & Holford 274 in 1966)			
138	(108)	with O.G. Smith (44)	v Australia	Kingston	1954–5
		(record for West Indies v Australia until Kanhai & Murray 165 in 1972–3)			

Walcott featured altogether in 17 century partnerships in Tests for the West Indies. His average of one century partnership for every 4.35 innings in Test cricket is good, although it does not compare favourably with Headley's 3.63 (11 in 40), Sobers's 3.63 (44 in 160) or Weekes's 3.85 (21 in 81). Walcott shared five of these stands with Worrell, 4 with Weekes, 3 with Sobers and 2 with Gomez.

WORLD AND WEST INDIAN RECORDS STILL STANDING

Although Walcott has been retired from first-class cricket for more than thirty years, several of his records still remain intact. The following are some of the most significant:

1. 5 centuries in a single Test series, against Australia in 1954–5

2. Separate centuries in a Test match twice in the same series, against Australia 1954–5.

3. Most runs ever scored against Australia in a Test series abroad, 827 in 1954–5.

4. Most runs ever scored in a Test series in the West Indies, 827 against Australia 1954–5.

5. Most Test centuries ever scored at Kingston, 5 (shared with G.St.A. Sobers).

6. Highest score ever made for Barbados against Trinidad, 314* in 1945–6.

7. Highest score ever made for Barbados, 314* against Trinidad, 1945–6.

8. Highest score ever made for West Indians v Tasmania, 186 in 1951–2.

9. Highest score ever made for West Indians v Wellington, 148 in 1951–2.

10. Record 4th wicket partnership for Barbados, 574* with F.M.M. Worrell, v Trinidad, 1946.

11. Record 5th wicket partnership for Barbados, 222 with D.St.E. Atkinson v Trinidad, 1951.

12. Record 2nd wicket partnership for Barbados v British Guiana, 175 with R.E. Marshall, 1950.

13. Record 4th wicket partnership for Barbados v British Guiana, 227 with E.D. Weekes, 1950.

14. Record 3rd wicket partnership for British Guiana v Jamaica, 126* with R.B. Kanhai, 1960. (equalled by T. Mohammed and R.C. Fredericks in 1979–80).

15. Record 2nd wicket partnership for West Indians v Tasmania, 281 with F.M.M. Worrell, 1951–2.

16. Record 5th wicket partnership for West Indies v New Zealand, 189 with F.M.M. Worrell, 1951–2.

17. Record 4th wicket partnership for West Indies v India, 267 with G.E. Gomez, 1948–9.

18. Record 3rd wicket partnership for West Indians v Ceylon, 258 with E.D. Weekes, 1948–9.

19. Record 4th wicket partnership for West Indians v Surrey, 279 with R.E. Marshall, 1950.

20. Most stumpings by a West Indian in Test cricket, 11.

RECORD FOR ENFIELD IN THE LANCASHIRE LEAGUE

(BATTING)

Season	I	NO	Runs	Ave
1951	23	7	1136	71.00
1952	20	8	955	79.58
1953	21	10	1117	101.54
1954	19	5	783	55.92
TOTAL	**83**	**30**	**3991**	**75.30**

(BOWLING)

Season	O	M	R	W	Ave
1951	303.3		1032	53	19.47
1952	215.3		710	44	16.13
1953	260		707	52	13.59
1954	233.3		511	72	7.09
TOTAL	**1012.1**		**2960**	**221**	**13.39**